The Traditional Co… …ers Guild

BOOK of RECIPES

Desna Greenhow

Illustrations by Sheila Stafford

Julia

Location Map

1 Crowdy Mill, Totnes, Devon.
2 Otterton Mill, Devon.
3 Clapton Mill, Somerset.
4 Cann Mills, Shaftesbury, Dorset.
5 Headley Mill, Bordon, Hants.
6 Blackland Mill, Calne, Wilts.
7 Mapledurham, Oxfordshire.
8 Skenfrith Mills, Abergavenny.
9 Y-Felin, St. Dogmaels, Cardigan, Dyfed.
10 Charlecote Mill, Warwickshire.
11 Downfield Windmill, Soham, Cambs.
12 Newnham Mill, Tenbury Wells, Worcs.
13 Maxey Mill, Peterborough, Cambs.
14 Maud Foster Windmill, Boston, Lincs.
15 Muncaster Mill, Cumbria.
16 Little Salkeld Mill, Cumbria.

Metric Conversion Table

As all the recipes are in pounds and ounces, here is a conversion table to grammes, kilogrammes and litres.

1 oz	—	29 gm
2 oz	—	58 gm
4 oz	—	115 gm
8 oz	—	230 gm
12 oz	—	345 gm
1 lb	—	460 gm
2.2 lb	—	1 kg
500 gms	—	1.1 lb
1.1 lb	—	500 gm
9 fl oz	—	250 ml (¼ lt)
18 fl oz	—	500 ml (½ lt)
1¾ pt	—	1 lt
1 pt	—	⅜ lt

Temperature

Gas Mark	°F	°C
4	350	180
5	375	190
6	400	205
7	425	220
8	450	230

Preface

The Traditional Corn Miller's Guild was formed at a meeting held at Mapledurham watermill, on the Thames, on a snowy Saturday in March 1987. The Guild members are all wind- and water-millers, running their mills directly for their own support and using primarily natural power to produce stoneground meals and flours. Apart from providing the growing band of small, independent millers with regular opportunities to meet and to discuss matters and problems of mutual interest, the Guild aims to promote the products of its members by educating and stimulating public interest. This recipe book is the first step at such promotion. At a time when public awareness is probably greater than ever concerning the quality of basic foodstuffs and the use of artificial additives and preservatives, the Traditional Corn Millers' Guild feels it necessary to emphasise the value of its members' products – unadulterated stoneground meals and flours.

The mills which comprise the Guild are spread throughout Britain and while each has its own range of stoneground products, the aim of all the millers is basically the same: straightforward, traditional quality. Most small millers use a high proportion of locally grown, English wheat and work as craftsmen, using traditional machinery and methods to give a product of great interest and quality. Stoneground flour milling is not an anachronism; there is already some awareness of the individual flavour and texture that stoneground flour gives to cooking, as well as the high food value. In addition, stoneground flour has an aesthetic quality which is found lacking in most mass-produced foods. In this book Desna Greenhow has put together many recipes which will show just how widely a simple product such as flour can be used and with such pleasing results.

Martin Watts
Chairman, TCMG

1. Bread and Rolls

Making good bread depends very much on the quality of the flour, as that is its main ingredient. Yeast breads need high gluten levels if they are to rise successfully, and high protein levels to give them flavour and make them nourishing. Traditional millers meet these requirements (for requirements they are when we are aiming to produce satisfying loaves which can be meals in themselves) in several different ways. English milling wheats have been bred to grow well in our uncertain summers in the last few years, and varieties of winter wheat such as Avalon and spring wheat such as Timmo and Sicco often pass the tests people are normally looking for of 12% protein. On the other hand it is not possible to expect that a farmer who has grown good milling wheat one year will do so the next, because our wind-swept island varies its weather so unpredictably from valley to valley, and from summer to summer. With this in mind, some millers mix native wheat with Canadian, grown in the big North American plains, and do not bother with searching for English grain which has passed the Hagburg test for gluten with flying colours. Nevertheless, to find high quality wheat which has been grown in one's own neighbourhood has its own reward. The harvesting, milling and baking processes have once again been brought down into the confines of an area, and a certain individuality must result. Many millers, too, meet the requests of their customers for organically grown grains. It is the various ways that millers meet these and other problems which makes for a welcome variety of loaf from different flours. Some mills are conscious of the extra lightness to be obtained from finely ground wholemeals, others of the extra richness and flavours to be found in malted meals. In this section you will find recipes for wheat breads, our most common staple, and for bread from other grains such as rye and barley which are also ground in some of our mills.

Hundred Percent Wholemeal Bread

Wholemeal flour (or wholewheat flour) is so-called because the whole of the wheat grain is in it. Nothing is added, by law, and nothing taken away. Most traditional mills make more wholemeal flour than any other kind. There is a list of those of us who do at the end of the book. Stone grinding produces a nutty flavoured meal which may be coarse or fine, according to the demands of the customers and the skills of the miller. The wheat oil is gently released by the warm, but not hot friction generated between the stones, and none of the nutriments are killed by over-heating.

3lb. 100% wholemeal flour
2oz. yeast
1 dstsp. salt
1 dstsp. brown sugar
1¾ pts. water

N.B Flour is usually packed in 1.5 kg. bags, or 3.3 lb. 1 packet is therefore the right amount for this recipe, with just enough flour over to flour your tins and work surface

Put the flour and salt in to a warm place in a large mixing bowl while you crumble the fresh yeast into a smaller bowl with the sugar, and add about ¾pt. of water, warmed to blood heat. (You should be able to put your elbow into the water without it feeling hot or cold). After about ten minutes in a fairly warm place, your yeast mixture will be frothing and sizzling. Be careful not to put it onto the stove, or let it get hot, or the yeast will be killed and you will not be able to raise your loaf. Now add the yeast mixture to the warmed flour, mixing with your hand. Continue adding the rest of the warm water (1¾ pints in all) until you have a dough. It will be considerably wetter than a white bread dough, and you mix it with your hands until it has a life of its own and will come away from the sides of the bowl. Do not knead it, but cover it with a piece of clingfilm, and put it once again in a fairly warm place to rise for about half an hour. While you are waiting, oil and flour your tins. You can use loaf tins, two 2 pounders for this amount of dough, or you can bake flowerpot loaves, or shape your loaves and cook them on a baking sheet with shallow sides to prevent them spreading too much. When the dough has risen, divide and weigh it, and then shape it on a floured surface. You knead it at this point, but do not overdo it or a lively dough can become dead and heavy. Leave the loaves for ten minutes in the tins, and then bake in a really hot oven, about 450 degrees, for 35-40 minutes. Tip loaves out of their tins and cook upside down for the last ten minutes. When the bread comes out of the oven, let it cool on wire trays, so that it does not become soggy.

Bread Animals Children love making these.

Here is the way to make some of the animals which can be found round a mill. You need to work with pieces of dough about the size of two grownup fists.

Millstream Eel

Get a piece of dough about the size of two fists. Roll it between your two hands until it is long and eel-like. Put it into a piece of greaseproof paper, and give it a few wriggles in its body. Give it two currant eyes.

Mouse

Shape a piece of dough to make a mouse, with pointy nose and humpty back. Keep back three small pieces for his ears and his long tail. (Do not make it too thin, or it will break off in the baking). Set him on a piece of greaseproof paper, and give him currant eyes.

Spider

Divide your dough into five, one big piece, and four small pieces. Shape the big piece into a nice big spider body. Then roll out the four small pieces, and press them onto the back of his body so that the ends stick out at each side for his legs. (Spiders have eight legs). Give him currant eyes, and a mouth, if you like.

Dove

Divide your dough into two pieces, one a little bigger than the other. Shape the bigger piece into your dove's body, like this. With a pair of scissors, make four snips at the bottom of the dough, for his tail. Put the second piece of dough crosswise, behind the first, bending down the ends for his wings. Give him eyes, and put him on a piece of greaseproof.

Whichever animal you make, leave it on its piece of greaseproof to rise for about half an hour, and bake in a really hot oven (about 450 degrees) for quarter of an hour. (It will not need as long as a loaf of bread, as it is smaller).

I hope you enjoy eating your own bread animal for tea.

Hosken's Mill Wholemeal Bread

Mr. and Mrs. Hoskens produce a strong Baker's Grade 100% stoneground flour, available in 32 kg., 15 kg. and 1.5 kg. bags. Malted wheat flakes are also available. Their flour is made from 75% Canadian Wheat and 25% English.

(For 10 loaves)

9lbs. stoneground wholemeal flour	*12 tsps. salt*
3lbs. malted wheat flakes	*½ pt. oil*
6 pkts. 'Easy Bake' dried yeast	*6 pts. warm water*

Mix dry ingredients, and then add oil and water. Mix either by hand or in mixer with a dough hook. Mould into tin size, and allow to rise in the tins for 1 hour. Bake in a hot oven for 30 minutes.

Sour Dough Bread

This is a pioneering bread made first by European immigrants in the United States, where it is still popular. It illustrates how wholemeal bread can be made to rise, using its own wild yeasts. The process is more like beer-making than bread making, but the end result is a dense, filling bread with a strong taste of its own.

3lb. wholemeal flour
5 onions
1 tsp. cumin seeds
(1/2 tsp. chilli powder (optional)).
Approx. 1 pt. water

Make a starter of 4oz. flour with 4 oz. warm water. Leave it uncovered, at room temperature, for two and a half days, stirring occasionally, and adding water if it is getting dry. By the end of this time, it should be bubbly, smell yeasty, and have increased in volume. Chop the onions, liquefy them in a liquidizer (or grate them), and add them with the cumin and chilli (if used) to the starter, with the rest of the warm water. Leave for about twelve hours. Now mix in the rest of the flour, which you have warmed. You are looking for a stiff dough, which requires kneading. It may take half an hour to incorporate all the flour. Let it rise in a warm place for two to three hours, under clingfilm and then shape it into three oval or round loaves. Rise again, covered, for five hours more. Brush with water, and bake in a hot oven for 50 minutes, lowering the heat and brushing again with water for the last 20 minutes. It sounds laborious, but if you time it so that you add the onion mixture in the evening, leave it overnight, do your kneading in the morning, and your rising through that day, you can bake the bread for supper.

Granary Loaf

One or two traditional millers produce a granary flour (Nick Jones at Little Salkeld Mill, nr. Penrith, and Norman Stoate at Cann Mills, Shaftesbury, for instance) but you can make up a granary meal yourself without much trouble, if you find it difficult to buy, to make this delicious kind of loaf, which has become so popular recently.

1 lb. wholemeal flour
2 oz. rye flour
4 oz. cracked wheat
1 tsp. salt
1/2 oz. fresh yeast
1 tsp. brown sugar
1 oz. black treacle
3/1 pt. warm water

Warm your mixing bowl with the flours and the cracked wheat and salt in it. Cream your yeast with the brown sugar, and about 1/4 pt. of the warm water. Add to the flours, and keep adding the rest of the water, with the black treacle in it, until you have a dough which comes away from the side of the bowl. Leave to rise, covered with clingfilm for about 45 minutes. Shape and knead a little. Form into two round or oval loaves. Brush with water, and sprinkle with cracked wheat. Bake for 30 minutes at 450 degrees. Cool on a wire tray.

Little Salkeld Soda Bread

Nick Jones, at Little Salkeld Mill, nr. Penrith, produces 100% and 85% plain and self-raising wheat flours, 100% rye flour, 85% barley flour, a 50% Canadian organic blend for bread making, a 50% Canadian non-organic blend,

'Water-mill' blend, including soya, sunflower and sesame, 'Granarious', a granary type and various grades of oatmeal. Most meals are from organically grown crops.

2lb. wholewheat flour
½ oz. salt or kelp powder
2 tsps. baking powder or 1 tsp. each of cream of tartar and bicarbonate of soda.
2 oz. melted butter or vegetable margarine
1 pt. milk (preferably sour)

Mix the flour, salt and baking powder in a bowl. Make a well in the middle and add the melted fat and milk. Mix quickly and lightly. Divide the dough into two and shape into loaves. Place on a floured baking sheet or into bread tins and brush with milk. Bake at 400 degrees F. (Gas Mark 6) for 45 minutes.

N.B. Too much salt is now agreed to put a strain on the kidneys by increasing our craving for liquids and it may also contribute to various circulatory diseases. By substituting kelp powder, a good flavour is added to this bread, and it also contains iodine, which some vegetarians lack in their diet. It may be used in other recipes too.

Little Salkeld Mill, Nr. Penrith, Cumbria.
Granite burr stones are powered by the River Eden.

Whole Wheat Grain Bread

You may find the occasional whole grain of wheat in stoneground flour, which has bounced onto the top of the stone instead of going into the hole (or eye) in the cente, and so missed being ground. Some people mind this more than others. Here is a recipe which uses whole grains intentionally, though they are simmered first to soften them.

3 oz. wheat, simmered for about 2½ hours in 1 pt. water (add more water as necessary)
½ pt. warm milk
1½ oz. fresh yeast
4 tblsps. honey
2 tblsps. melted butter
2 tsps. salt
1½ lb. whole wheat flour
2 oz. wheat germ, softened in the honey

Cream the yeast with about quarter of a pint of the water in which the wheat is simmered, cooled down with milk to blood heat, and with about a tblsp. of honey Mix flour, wheat germ and salt. Add melted butter to the creamed yeast, and mix the yeast liquid into the flour. Add the rest of the wheat water and milk, mixed to make a liquid that is blood heat. Finally add the wheat grains and mix until the dough leaves the sides of the bowl. Cover with clingfilm and rise for forty minutes, or until it is double in size. Shape and knead on a floured board, and divide into two loaves. Bake at 450 degrees for 40 minutes. Turn out and bake upside down on the shelf for the last ten minutes.

Wheat Sprout Bread

Sprout wheat grains as you would alfalfa or mung beans, for four days. Make loaves using the above method and quantities, but mixing warm water and milk for the liquid. Incorporate the sprouted wheat into the dough instead of the simmered grain. A moist and nutty flavoured loaf will be the result.

Wholemeal Bread Sticks

1½ oz. fresh yeast
¾ pt. warm water
1 tsp. salt
1 dstsp. brown sugar
1½ lb. wholemeal flour
Beaten egg
Coarse sea salt

Cream yeast with warm water and sugar. Mix with the flour and salt to make a fairly stiff dough. Turn onto a floured board, and knead. Divide into 48 pieces (approx.) and roll each into a rope ½ inch in diameter and 9 inches long. Place on oiled baking sheets. Brush with beaten egg and sprinkle generously with coarse sea salt. Bake at 425 degrees for 12 to 15 minutes, or until brown.

Cann Mills Wholemeal Rolls

Norman and Michael Stoate, at Cann Mills, nr. Shaftesbury, produce plain, organic, self-raising and extra strong flours in 100% and 81% extraction, as well as Maltsar (a granary type) and rye flour.

For 18 rolls (scaled at 3 oz.)
2 lb. 81% or 100% stoneground flour
½ oz. salt
2 oz. fresh yeast
1½ oz. lard
½ oz. brown sugar
1 pt. water

Put the flour and salt into a mixing bowl and mix. Flour will be very much warmer in summer than in winter, and it is necessary to counteract the seasonable variations in temperature by the heat of the water added, and by leaving the dough to ferment in a warmer or cooler environment. You may take the temperature of the flour at this point. Rub the fat into the flour and salt. Dissolve the sugar and yeast in ¾ of the water. Pour the liquid into the mixing bowl and start mixing and kneading. Your dough can be slightly sticky. Leave the dough covered in its bowl in a warm place for 30 minutes. Lightly knead the dough and then divide into 3 oz. pieces. Mould into rounds and place onto trays. Cover and leave to prove in a warm place until well risen. Bake at 460 degrees for 12-15 minutes.

Otterton Mill Rolls

Desna Greenhow, at Otterton Mill, nr. Budleigh Salterton produces a 100% wholemeal flour, and own label baked goods using this, and flours bought from other traditional millers.

2 lb. wholemeal flour
1 pt. milk
2 oz. yeast
3 eggs
1 tsp. brown sugar
1 tsp. salt

Cream the yeast with the sugar, in a little water. Mix flour and salt. Warm milk and add beaten eggs to it, being careful to warm it to blood heat again afterwards. Mix liquid into the flour, and rise for 30 minutes. Knead on a floured board, adding a little flour if necessary, to make a dough which can be handled. Shape into 4 oz. rounds, and space on a baking tray so that they just join up when they have proved. Bake for 12-15 minutes at 450 degrees, having brushed them over with beaten egg before putting them in the oven. The above quantities makes 16 rolls. Cool on a wire tray.

Plaited Harvest Loaf

This loaf is a lovely golden colour, suitable for harvest festival. It tastes good, too.

1 oz. fresh yeast
¼ pt. warm water
1 dstsp. brown sugar
½ oz. butter
½ pt. warm milk
1 dstsp. sea salt
1 tblsp. honey
2 eggs
1½ lb. wholemeal flour
2 tblsp. wheat germ
Beaten egg for glazing
Sesame seeds or poppy seeds

Crumble the yeast into the warm water with the brown sugar. Weigh out the flour, and stand in a warm place, having added the wheat germ and sea salt. Warm the milk, honey and butter to blood heat. Add the two beaten eggs, and warm again a little. When the yeast is working, add the yeast mixture to the flour, combining them thoroughly but gently. Add the egg and milk mixture gradually, mixing until you have a dough which comes away easily from the sides of the bowl. Leave the bowl in a fairly warm place, covered with clingfilm to rise for about half an hour. Turn the dough onto a floured board, and knead it for a few minutes. Now divide it into three equal pieces. Roll out each to a sausage, twelve inches long. With a little water, secure the three together at one end and then begin plaiting them firmly. When you reach the end, seal with water and turn both ends underneath the loaf. Leave to rise for about ten minutes on a shallow baking tin. Brush with beaten egg, and scatter poppy seeds or sesame seeds over the loaf, before baking for 35 minutes at 450 degrees. Cool on a wire tray, handling with care until it is cold.

French Bread

Some breads can only be made from white flour, and many traditional mills produce unbleached, creamy coloured flour, excellent for such breads as French baguettes. (Some traditional millers who make these flours are Martin Watts at Crowdy Mill, James Waterfield at Maud Foster Mill, Peter Ellis at Muncaster Mill, Michael Hall at Y Felin Mill, Norman Stoate at Cann Mills, Nigel Moon at Downfield Windmills and Mildred Cookson at Mapledurham Mill).

2 oz. butter
1 tblsp. salt
1 tblsp. sugar
¾ pt. boiling water
2 oz. fresh yeast
¼ pt. warm water
1½ lb. unbleached, hard white flour
Corn meal

Combine the butter, salt, sugar and boiling water in a mixing bowl and stir until the butter is melted and the sugar and salt dissolved. Cool to blood heat. Mix in the yeast, and add ¼ pt. warm water. Add the flour gradually until you have added 1 lb. Beat well with a wooden spoon for about ten minutes. Continue adding flour until you have a stiff dough. Turn onto a floured board, and knead until the dough is smooth and elastic. Form into a ball and cover. Leave in a warm place to rise for 1½ hours. Knock back, and then rise for another hour. Oil a baking sheet, and sprinkle with corn meal. Divide dough into three. Roll each into a rectangle, 14″ × 8″. Now make tight rolls so that each loaf is 1½ inches wide. Pinch the seam and the ends and place on the baking tray. Cover with clingfilm and rise until they are twice the size. Brush the tops with cold water and make three diagonal slashes across them with a sharp knife. Bake at 400 degrees for 50 minutes, with a shallow pan of hot water in the oven. Brush the loaves with more cold water every twenty minutes, to get a hard crust. Stand them on end soon after taking them out of the oven.

Crusty White Bread

1½ lb. unbleached white flour
1 tsp. sea salt
1 tsp. brown sugar
1½ oz. fresh yeast
¼ pt. warm water
2 oz. melted butter or
3 tblsps. oil
8 fl.oz. warm milk
1 egg, lightly beaten

Cream yeast with sugar in warm water and add butter or oil and milk. Combine with flour and salt, and knead well. Cover and rise for 1½ hours. Knock back and knead again. Cut in half and roll each half into a rectangle 8 inches by 10 inches. Roll them up like swiss rolls, tucking the ends in. Put on the oiled baking sheet to rise again for 40 minutes. Slash the tops diagonally, brush with a little milk and beaten egg. Rise for another hour, then bake at 400 degrees for 30 minutes, with a pan of hot water in the oven. Brush with cold water after 15 minutes. Cool on a wire tray.

Cann Mill Baps

2 lb. 81% stoneground flour
1 oz. salt
1½ oz. lard
3 oz. fresh yeast
½ oz. white sugar
1 pt. (approx.) half water, half milk

Put the flour and salt into a mixing bowl and mix. Rub the fat with the flour and salt. Dissolve the sugar and yeast in ¾ of the required water. Pour the liquid into the mixing bowl and start mixing and kneading. Add more water until the dough is smooth and elastic. Leave covered in its bowl in a warm place for 30 minutes. Lightly knead the dough, then mould into 3 oz. rounds as if making rolls, then use a rolling pin to roll them out flat. Place on a greased baking tray and leave covered in a warm place to prove as normal. When well risen dust with flour before baking for 12-15 minutes at 460 degrees F.

Here are three breads we are used to seeing in specialist shops and bakeries, but which can easily be made at home.

Vienna Rolls

2 lb. finest unbleached white flour
1½ oz. fresh yeast
½ oz. salt
¾ pt. milk
¼ pt. water
1 tsp. sugar

Cream yeast with ¼ pt. warm water, and the same amount of warm milk. Make a stiff dough with ⅓ of the flour, and the yeast mixture. Put in a warm place to rise for half an hour. Mix the remainder of the flour with the rest of the liquid, and add the risen dough. Knead well. Rise for an hour, then knock back. Divide into 4 oz. balls. Rise for another hour then place on a baking tray. Brush with yolk of egg, and bake at 375 degrees for 12-15 minutes.

Pitta Bread

These are good split open and filled with various mixtures, such as kebabs and yoghurt or mayonnaise and tuna. They make a lunch which is more filling than a sandwich.

1 25 mg. ascorbic acid tablet
½ pt. warm milk
1 oz. fresh yeast
1 oz. margarine
1 lb. strong unbleached white flour
1 tsp. sugar
1 tsp. salt

Crush the vitamin tablet and mix with the crumbled yeast into the warm milk. Rub the fat into the flour, mix in sugar and salt. Make a well in the middle and add the yeast mixture. Add the rest of the milk to make a firm dough. Knead on a floured board for ten minutes. Rise in a warm place, covered, for twenty minutes. Knead again, then divide into twelve. Shape each piece into a flat oval and put, well apart, onto baking trays. Cover in clingfilm, loosely, and rise until they are double in size. Brush with beaten egg and bake for 12-15 minutes at 400 degrees.

Chapattis

8 oz. wheatmeal flour
2 tsps. oil
¼ pt. water

Sift the flour into a bowl, add the oil and gradually mix in the water to make a soft dough. Knead for a few minutes, then set aside for half an hour. Break off small pieces of dough and roll out on a floured board into thin circles. Cook on a hot griddle or heavy frying pan for a few seconds on each side. Hold with tongs over a gas flame, or finish under a hot grill. Chapattis are served with many Indian dishes. (Charlecote Mill in Warwickshire specializes in a wholemeal flour of English wheat, suitable for wholemeal chapattis (AEC)).

Oaten Bread

Oatmeal is ground in greater quantities in Wales and Scotland than in England, and some traditional millers in all these countries produce it. Oatcake, cooked on a griddle or in the oven, is the old-fashioned bread eaten in the Celtic countries. (Traditional mills which grind oatmeal include Little Salkeld, North Leverton Windmill, Downfield Windmill and Y Felin Mill (Cardigan)).

Scotch Oakcake

1 lb. medium oatmeal
2 tblsp. melted bacon fat or butter
1 dstsp. sea salt
Boiling water

Mix salt and oatmeal, and pour in the fat, melted in some of the water. Work and knead, adding more water to form a soft dough. Roll out as thinly as possible on a board sprinkled with fine oatmeal. Cut into squares or triangles, and bake in a cool oven, or on a griddle, until they begin to curl. Dry in a very cool oven, or in front of a fire.

Oatmeal Bread

½ pt. boiling water
6 oz. oatmeal
2 oz. brown sugar
2 oz. butter
2 tsps. sea salt
1½ oz. fresh yeast
1¼ pt. warm water (approx)
1½ lb. unbleached white flour

Pour the boiling water over the oatmeal, and stand for 30 minutes. Add the brown sugar, butter and salt. Cream the yeast with the warm water, and add. Work in the flour until you have a medium soft dough. Knead on a floured board. Cover and rise for about 45 minutes. Knead again, and shape into two loaves Turn into loaf tins, and rise again for 30 minutes. Bake for 45 minutes at 400 degrees, moving the loaves lower down in the oven after 15 minutes. Brush the tops of the loaves with butter, for a soft crust.

Mixed Whole Grain Bread

1 oz. fresh yeast
4 fl. oz. warm water
1 tsp. brown sugar
½ pt. warm milk
1 tblsp. sea salt
½ oz. butter
10 oz. wholemeal flour
7 oz. rye flour
7 oz. oatmeal
1 egg

Cream the yeast, warm water and sugar. Mix the milk and butter until the butter melts. Add the beaten egg. Combine the flours and salt, and warm in the mixing bowl. Make a hole in the middle and add the liquids, mixing well until the mixture leaves the sides of the bowl. Leave to rise in a warm place, covered with clingfilm for 35 minutes. Knead a little on a floured board, and shape into a 2 lb. loaf. Rise a little longer in the loaf tin. Sprinkle with medium oatmeal and bake at 400 degrees for one hour. Cool on a wire rack. Do not cut until it is cold. Very delicious.

Low Gluten Bread

Some people are allergic to wheat, at least to the gluten in wheat. Try the following mixed grain loaf. You can also try combining soya and rice flours, and using the same technique.

2 oz. fresh yeast
4 fl. oz. warm water
½ pt.. warm milk
1 tblsp. sea salt or kelp
½ oz. butter or vegetable margarine
7 oz. peasemeal
7 oz. rye flour
10 oz. oatmeal
3 eggs

Use the same method as for the Mixed Whole Grain Bread, above.

Barley Bread

Barley flour is often ground for animal feed by traditional millers, but it can make a loaf with a distinctive flavour of its own. Oven-baked barley bread is usually mixed with wheat flour to give it a better colour and to tone down its strong flavour, but this griddle-baked loaf, quickly made for days when everyone was in the harvest fields and there was no time to bake, is well worth a try as well.

Barley Griddle Bread

1 lb. barley flour
4 oz. unbleached white flour
1 tsp. sea salt
1 tsp. bicarbonate of soda
2 tsps. cream of tartar
1 pt. buttermilk (obtainable from Sainsbury's)

Mix the dry ingredients together. Stir in the buttermilk to make a light firm dough. Do not take too long over the mixing. Speed is everything. Shape into a round cake 1 inch thick, and cook quickly on a hot griddle or heavy frying pan, turning it over once the first side is cooked. Alternatively, bake at 475 degrees for 20 minutes, on a greased baking sheet, without turning.

Rye Bread

Rye has never been the most popular grain crop of these islands. Iron age farming did not include it, and rye bread, in the middle ages was what the peasant ate, while he sold his valuable wheat crop to buy necessities. Several of our traditional mills grind rye, and it is a bread which has become in demand since people became more adventurous in their diets. (Amongst the mills producing rye flour are Crowdy Mill, Little Salkeld Mill, Maud Foster Mill, Y Felin Mill, Cann Mills and Downfield Windmill). Rye flour has less gluten than most wheat flours and is almost always mixed with wheat flour to help it to rise.

Rye Bread

½ pt. scalded milk
¼ pt. warm water
2 tsps. honey
1½ oz. fresh yeast
8 oz. rye flour
14 oz. wholemeal flour (high gluten)
2 tsps. salt
1 tblsp. caraway seeds (optional)

Scald the milk, then leave it to cool to blood heat. Cream the yeast with the warm water and honey. Mix flours and salt together and warm them. Mix in the yeast mixture and then add the milk, until you have a fairly stiff dough. Mix in the caraway seeds, if used. Knead on a floured board for ten minutes. cover and put in a warm place to rise until it is twice the size. Knock it back, and knead again. Rise it again. (The second rising is important with rye bread, as it will not rise as easily as a wheaten loaf). Divide the dough into two 1 lb. loaves, or make a single 2 lb. loaf. It is better baked in tins, to help it keep its shape. Sprinkle the top with caraway seeds, having brushed it with beaten egg. Bake for 40 minutes at 400 degrees.

Pumpernickel

Many of the more interesting rye loaves originate from the continent and pumpernickel comes from Germany, as its name suggests. It is a delicious dark loaf, very high in protein.

½ oz. fresh yeast
3 tblsps. warm water
1 oz. butter
½ oz. caraway seeds
2 tblsp. sea salt
2 tblsps. brown sugar
1½ oz. currants
¾ pt. scalded milk
½ lb. rye flour
10 oz. wholemeal flour (high gluten)
2 oz. bran
2 oz. wheat germ
The grated rind of two lemons

Cream the yeast in the warm water with the sugar. Put the butter, caraway seeds, lemon peel, salt and currants into your mixing bowl and pour the scalded milk over them. Cool to blood heat, then mix in the yeast liquid, the rye flour and half the wholemeal flour. Beat with a wooden spoon, adding the bran and wheat germ. Turn the dough onto a well-floured board, and add the rest of the wholemeal as you knead, so as to prevent the mixture getting sticky. Put the lump of dough back into the bowl to rise in a warm place, covered, for 1½ hours. Knock it back and roll it like a swiss roll. Pinch the seam and the ends to keep in the air, and allow to rise on a floured baking sheet for about an hour, until double in size. Brush with cold water and bake at 400 degrees for 50 minutes. Brush again with cold water once during the baking after 35 minutes.

Limpa, or Swedish Rye Bread

½ pt. pale ale
½ lb. coarse rye flour
1 pt. milk
1½ oz. yeast
1½ lb. unbleached high gluten white flour
½ lb. treacle
1 dstsp. fennel (chopped)
1½ oz. butter
The chopped rind of 1 orange

Warm the ale and put into a pudding basin with the rye flour. Work for 10 minutes, and stand for 12 hours. Cream the yeast with the warm milk, and add to the rye mixture with the white flour. Mix well and leave to rise in a warm place until it is double the size. Work in the treacle, chopped fennel and orange peel, and more white flour, if necessary, to make a very stiff dough. Knead it well, and leave it to rise again for 1½ hours or until it is double in size again. Shape as for pumpernickel, and allow to rise once more. Brush with cold water and bake at 400 degrees for 40 minutes, brushing twice with cold water during the baking.

Hosken's Mill,
Blackland,
Nr. Calne, Wilts.

The River Marden
powers 3 pairs of
French burr stones.

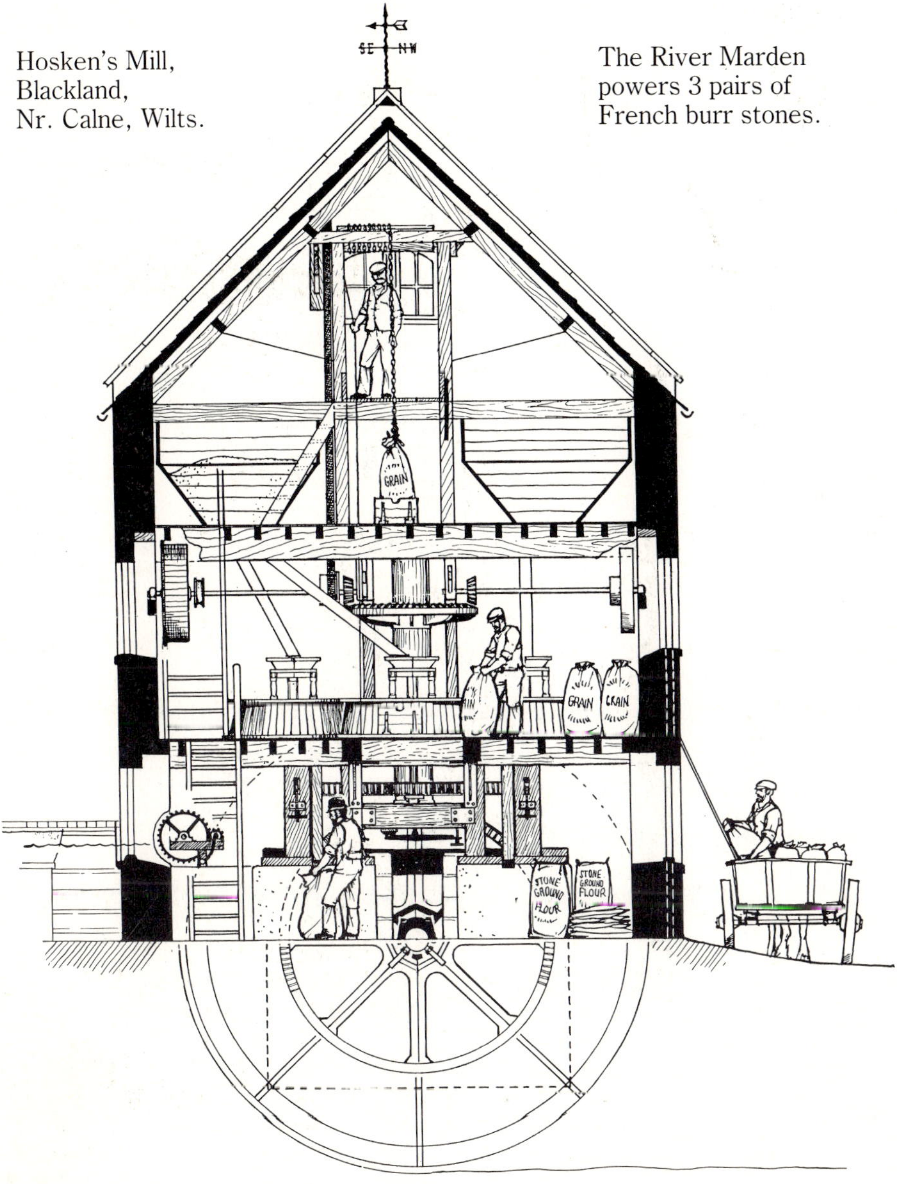

2. Fish and Meat Main Courses

In these islands we have a long tradition of using pastry, batters and suet crusts to add warming bulk to fish and meat dishes. Wheat flour is the basic ingredient for all of these, and some millers produce soft wheat flours specially for this kind of baking. However, it is best to use a harder flour for the pastries and batters which need to stand, and a soft flour for short crust, for instance, which must be made at speed.

Pizzas have also become an integral part of our cuisine, and some recipes are given here for making pizza dough. Also there are one or two recipes for using other flours than wheaten. Finnish rye flour pastry, for instance.

We also use breadcrumbs in some of our traditional meat loafs, and in stuffings for meat and poultry.

Lastly, here are a few oddities. Mill streams often abound with trout and with eels and elvers. Some of you may have a chance to fish in one. Only please not in my millstream where the trout at least are almost family pets, often rescued by my children when a sudden downpour silts up the sluice gates, and the mill stream suddenly empties out!

Pastry Cooking

My mother was brought up in a mill house on the River Kent, in what was then Westmorland. Granny prided herself on her scrubbed flagstones, and her pastry. She passed her skills on to her daughters, and my mother gave me one of my earliest cookery lessons in the different kinds of pastry, and how to make them. Here, verbatim, is what she once wrote down.

Short Crust Pastry

To 1 lb. white flour, ½ lb. lard/butter (good fresh lard, and a speck or two of butter). 1 tsp. baking powder, ½ tsp. salt. Water.

Sieve the flour from a height. Rub in the fat. Add salt and baking powder. Mix well and add less water than you think (about ¼ of a pint minus). Try to do the rolling out in one Beetonish gesture. Never let the rolling pin go quite to the edge, because it would squeeze out the air that you've got in by seiving. Always cook at once at 400 degrees. Seconds count.

Flaky Pastry

To 8 oz. flour, 6 oz. lard/butter. A lemon. Water. 1 tsp. salt.

Seive the flour onto the table. Chop the fat into dice and roll them in the flour. Make a heap of this with a well in the middle, into which put 1 tsp. salt, the juice of the lemon and a dollop of water. Fight the thing with a knife, turning the dry outer rim into the centre puddle and scraping back escaping streams and preserving the lumps of fat intact. Make a fresh well, add some more water and mix again. If your fat is soft, make a wettish dough, if it is hard, use less water and make a stiff one. When the mass can be handled, flour it and roll it out (again, not quite to the edge). Fold into three and roll again – with the folded edges to right and left. Do this four times. *Then* roll it up and put it in a cool place for at least an hour, but the longer the better – say 24 if you like. Bake at 425 degrees.

Puff Pastry

While short crust and flaky work best with white flour, (and you can use brown as well, being careful to ask for a soft flour for shortcrust), puff pastry is delicious made with hard wholewheat flour.

8 oz. wholemeal of white unbleached flour to 8 oz. butter, or hard vegetable margarine. 1 tsp. salt. Water (up to ¼ of pint).

Seive the flour and salt into a bowl. Mix to a firm dough with the water. Place the butter or margarine, uncut, in the centre of the dough, and bring it up round the block, until you have a brick-shaped square. Leave, covered, in a cool place for ¼ of an hour. Turn out onto a floured surface, sprinkle very well with flour, and begin rolling into a triangle. Turn the corners of the triangle into the centre and roll again, trapping some air, and not rolling to the edges. Do this seven times, then roll the pastry up. You will want to incorporate quite a bit more flour as you roll, and as you come on areas of fat in the pastry. You may need almost as much again as you had in the original dough. Finally, roll the pastry in a floured cloth, and keep it in a cool place for at least an hour. Bake at 425-450 degrees.

Eel Pie

10 oz. flaky pastry made with white unbleached flour.
1½ lb. eel cut into 1 inch cubes, and skinned.
Eel trimmings
6 shallots
2 oz. butter
A small glass medium sherry
2 hard-boiled eggs
Juice of ½ a lemon
¼ pt. single cream
Fresh thyme
3 tblsps. fresh parsley
Salt and pepper

Simmer eel trimmings in water (¾ pt.) for 20 minutes. Soften the shallots in the butter, and add the eel pieces, coated in seasoned wholewheat flour. Cook them until lightly browned. Put eel and shallots on one side, and stir 1 tblsp. seasoned wholemeal flour into the juices in the pan. Cook for a minute, then add the stock made from the eel trimmings. Stir it well, and let it reduce for about 5 minutes on a hot ring. Add the sherry and cream, and adjust flavouring, adding lemon juice. Stir in the herbs. Allow to cool. Arrange all in a pie dish, topping with hard-boiled eggs, sliced. Cover with the flaky pastry, and bake at 425 degrees for 15 minutes. Cover with wet greaseproof paper, and cook for 20 minutes more at 350 degrees.

Fish and Pork Pie

½ lb. flaky pastry, made with half wheat flour/half rye flour and 6 oz. butter.
¾ lb. halibut steaks
6 oz. pork, not too lean
½ tsp. dill seed
Lemon juice
Salt and pepper
½ pt. water
1 large onion

Poach the fish in water with the onion, sliced, and the pared rind of half the lemon. Brown the pork in a tblsp. olive oil. Roll out the pastry, and line a pie dish with half of it. Put in a layer of fish, one of pork slices, sprinkle with dill seed and a little of the softened onion from the poaching of a the fish. Continue adding layers like this until the ingredients are used up. Pour over enough of the water used for poaching the fish to three quarters cover the mixture. Roll out the other half of the pastry, and lay on top of the pie. Moisten the edges to firmly seal top and bottom. Bake at 450 degrees for 20 minutes. Cover with wet greaseproof paper, and bake another 20 minutes at 350 degrees.

Haddock Quiche

One 9 inch pastry case, made from 10 oz. wholewheat puff pastry, baked blind for 10 minutes, covered with greasproof paper, weighed down with beans, at 400 degrees.

½ lb. finnan haddock
1 large avocado pear
½ pt. natural yoghurt
2 fl.oz. double cream
Sea salt, and black pepper
4 beaten eggs

Poach the fish in ½ pt. water. Cool, and remove the skin and bones. Beat the eggs, and mix with the flaked fish, yoghurt and cream. Season well with salt and pepper. Pour into the flan case, and slice the avocado pear into long, thin slices. Arrange on top in a spoke shape. Bake at 375 degrees until the filling is set and pale brown (about 35 minutes).

Lakeland Fishy Pie

1 lb. smoked finnan haddock
½ pt. milk
1 oz. butter
1 oz. flour
2 hard-boiled eggs, coarsely chopped
1 tblsp. chopped parsley
Pepper
1¾ lb. shortcrust pastry, made with unbleached white flour

Poach haddock in a little of the milk. Cool a little, and remove bones and skin. Then flake the fish. Melt butter in a pan. Add flour and cook a minute without browning. Make fish liquor up to ½ pt. with milk. Remove pan from heat and gradually add milk and fish liquor. Return to heat, bring to the boil, stirring until thickened. Remove from the heat and stir in haddock, eggs, parsley and pepper. Cool. Make the shortchrust pastry and divide in half. Roll out both pieces into an oblong, 12 inches by 8 inches, and about ¼ inch thick. Cut out into two fish shapes using a 12 in oval serving plate as a guide. Press an upturned wire cooling tray onto one piece of pastry to resemble scales, shape the mouth and tail on both pastry ovals. Lift the plain pastry fish onto a greased baking sheet. Spread with fish mixture to within 1 inch of the edge. Brush edges with milk. cover with other half pastry fish, scale side up, and seal edges. Using a fork, make marks like fins round the edges. Form an eye with the pastry trimmings. Brush whole fish with beaten egg. Bake at 400 degrees for 20 minutes, then at 375 degrees for 20 minutes more.

Stargazey Pie

The idea of pilchards baked whole in a pie, with their heads sticking out at the edges so that their eyes gaze towards the stars is not as disgusting at it sounds. The whole fish is baked so as to keep in all the rich juices, and the bottom layer of the pastry is wider than the top, so as to make cutting easier.

The head is, of course discarded before a slice is served.

16 small fish, pilchards or large sprats
1½ lb. shortcrust pastry, made with unbleached white flour.
Salt and pepper
8 oz. white breadcrumbs
2 finely chopped onions
1 dstsp. made mustard
1 tblsp. parsley
1 dstsp. thyme
1 large cooking apple

Scale and gut the fish, removing the fins. Mix the breadcrumbs, onion, mustard, herbs and apple in a bowl. Season well, and add a little extra apple juice to moisten. Stuff the fish. Roll out a little over half of the pastry, and line a 9 inch fireproof plate, well greased. Arrange the fish in a circle, their heads pointing outwards. Measure from the centre to just below their heads, and roll out the remaining pastry, and cut a round twice this distance in diameter. Top the pie with this piece, and the fish will look a little as if they are tucked up in bed. Brush over with beaten egg and bake at 400 degrees for 20 minutes, and then at 350 degrees for 20 minutes more, wrapped in a piece of wet greasproof paper.

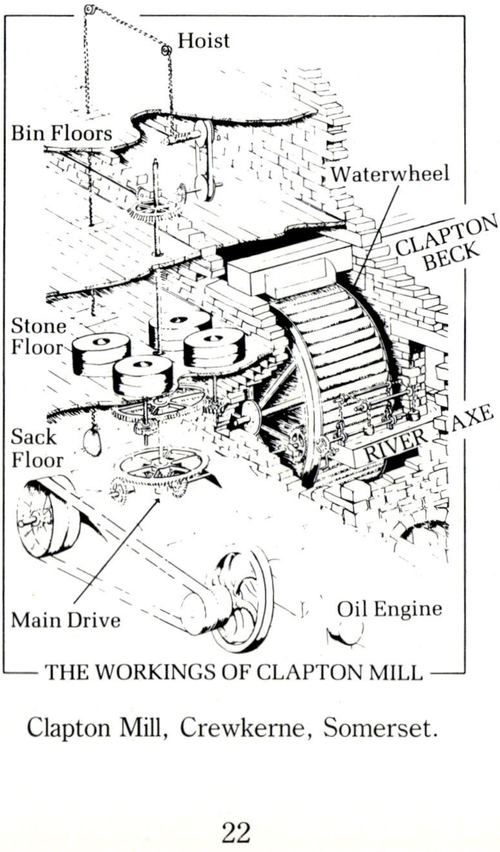

THE WORKINGS OF CLAPTON MILL

Clapton Mill, Crewkerne, Somerset.

Steak and Kidney Pie

Large savoury pies are an English speciality, and this one, or the chicken pie made by the same method, make as good a Sunday lunch as a joint of meat. The duck pie is a little more exotic, and more suitable for a party dish.

2 lb. lean stewing steak
1 tblsp. mixed thyme and parsley
¾ lb. ox kidney
2 onions
Seasoned flour
Water
½ lb. flaky pastry, made with unbleached white flour.

Cut up the beef and the kidney into pieces about 1 inch square, discarding any fat and the stringy core of the kidney. Slice the onions. Place in a large pie dish, and add seasoned flour and herbs, turning the pieces with your hands until all are coated. Three quarters fill the pie dish with water. Cover with foil and cook for 1½ hours at 325 degrees. Take out of the oven, and allow to cool. Forty minutes before you want to serve the pie, remove the foil, roll out the flaky pastry, and place on top of the pie, after placing an egg cup or a pie prop in the centre. You should line the edge of the pie dish with a thin strip of pastry, wetting it with water, and sticking firmly down. Roll the main pie crust so that it is bigger than the top of the dish, fold it in half, and put carefully onto one half of the dish. Unfold it so that it covers the pie. Stick with water to the edging strip, not stretching it too tightly. Trim off with a sharp knife. Brush with egg, mark the edges with a fork and prick a few holes in the crust, to form a pattern. Bake at 425 degrees for 20 minutes, then lower the heat to 350 for 20 minutes more, and keep an eye on it to see that it does not brown too much.

Chicken and Ham Pie

Make in exactly the same way as the steak and kidney pie, using one large chicken, jointed into seven pieces, and a thick half pound slice of shoulder ham, in place of the steak and kidney. Use stock made from the chicken carcase to moisten the meat in the first cooking.

Duck Pie

Joint a large duck and cut up 1 lb. lean pork, and ½ lb. lean bacon into 1 inch squares. Make a marinade from 2 onions, a bay leaf, 2 sprigs thyme, peppercorns, sea salt, 2 tsps. allspice, ½ a bottle of white wine, 1 tblsp. brandy. Marinade the meats for 24 hours, turning them over in the marinade from time to time. Make a rich stock with the duck carcase and pork bones. Skim it and reduce, so that it will set firmly. Cook as for Chicken and Ham and Steak and Kidney pie, but use your stock, with the liquid drained from the marinade, to cook the meats in. This pie may be eaten hot or cold.

Small Individual Pies

6 oz. wholewheat puff pastry. Make in individual foil pie dishes, lining with half the pasty, rolled thin. Wet the edges of top and bottom circles, and cover cooked ingredients with the seond half of pastry, rolled out to ¼ inch. Trim and mark with a fork round the edges and in the middle.

Venison Pies

Shoulder of venison. 1 shallot, unskinned. A small piece of nutmeg. Salt and pepper. Red currant or rowan jelly. Water. 6 oz. puff pastry. Cut the meat off the bones, and put the bones and trimmings into 1½ pts. water. Simmer for an hour, with the unskinned shallot. Fry venison meat lightly in 1 oz. butter, and season each piece in salt, pepper and nutmeg, grated. Put into the cooled stock, and simmer gently until the meat is tender. Take out the pieces of meat, wait until they have cooled a little, adjust seasoning and fill the individual pie cases you have lined with pastry. Cover as described above, and bake for 15 minutes at 425 degrees. When you take them out of the oven, slit the side of each, and pour in a tblsp. stock, and dstsp. of red currant jelly. Delicious eaten cold for a picnic lunch.

Mutton Spicey Pies

Make these mutton pies in exactly the same way using shoulder of lamb, and adding a sliced cooking apple to the meat to give it moisture in the cooking, instead of adding stock and jelly after it is cooked.

Hare Pies

Use the legs, back and front of a hare, and keep the saddle for another dish. Cook in the same way, using a cooking apple for moisture. Season with plenty of pepper.

Cornish Pasties

Here is a clerihew which sums up what many people think about Cornish pasties.

St. Just
Said 'The crust
Of this pasty
Is terribly nasty.'
His landlady cried
'Wait till you see the inside.'

A multitude of sins have been committed in the name of the Cornish pasty, still one of the most convenient portable lunches that there is, dating back to the British inhabitants of these islands, long before the days of St. Just. Good pasties are filling and delicious.

For 4 pasties:
2 lb. shortcrust pastry made with unbleached white flour
12 oz. chuck steak
8 oz. potatoes
1 turnip or half a swede
1 onion
Salt and pepper

Scrape the meat into *very* small slivers. (Do not mince, as it destroys the texture.) Grate the peeled potato and turnip or swede. Peel and finely chop the onion. Roll out the pastry and cut into four circles ⅛ inch thick, and 8 inches in diameter. Divide the meat between the circles, and top with the vegetables divided equally too. Season well with salt and pepper. Draw up the edges of the circles to make a seam across the top, pinching the edges together, and crimping them over to make a neat join. Brush with beaten egg, place on a greased baking sheet, and bake at 425 degrees for 15 minutes. Lower the heat to 325 degrees, and bake for 25-30 minutes more.

Raised Pies

These require a different kind of pastry, a hot water crust. Another kind of traditional English pie, needing either considerable skill, or a hinged pie mould, which you can buy at kitchen shops.

Hot Water Crust

For a pie for 4-6

7 oz. water
6 oz. lard
1 lb. white unbleached flour
½ tsp. salt
1 egg (optional)

Bring water and lard to the boil, and tip quickly into the flour and salt, waiting in a bowl. Mix at speed with a wooden spoon. Add the egg if you are using it. Allow to cool until it can be handled. Keep a quarter for the top, and use the rest to completely line a greased hinged pie mould. If it collapses, the pastry is still too hot, and you must wait a little.

Veal and Ham Pie

2 lb. stewing veal, cut in cubes
6 oz. uncooked shoulder ham, cut in cubes.
4 hard-boiled eggs
Jellied stock, made from veal trimmings and bone.
Seasoned flour
1 tsp. each of sage and marjoram

Roll the veal and ham in seasoned flour, fill the pastry case, made as above, dotting slices of hard-boiled egg at intervals. Moisten the edges, and roll out and fix the pastry crust on top. Decorate with pastry leaves and brush with beaten egg. Bake at 400 degrees for 30 minutes, then at 325 for 1½ hours. Cover with greaseproof paper if it browns too fast. Pour in warm stock when cooked. Allow to cool and set. Eat cold with mustard and a green salad.

Suet Crust and Dumplings

Suet crusts should be light and are normally used as pie toppings, as puddings completely surrounding the filling, and as rolls, as this recipe for mussel or oyster pudding, from the North East.

Mussel or Oyster Pudding

10 oz. self-raising unbleached white flour or plain flour mixed with 1 tsp. baking powder
½ tsp sea salt
5 oz. chopped fresh suet
6 oz. butter
Pepper
Chopped parsley and chives
5 doz. mussels or 2 doz. oysters
4-6 trimmed streaky bacon cut in strips
3 tblsps. chopped parsley
4½ oz. finely chopped onion

Mix flour, salt and suet together in a bowl with enough water to make a soft dough. Put in a cool place. Prepare the shell fish. If you are using mussels, scrub well, and open in a sauté pan with 4 tblsps. water. Heat them over a fierce heat for 40 seconds, and take them out as they open. If you are using oysters, open over a small pan, with an oyster knife, and then heat in their juice for a moment or two over moderate heat. Take the mussels or oysters out of their shells. Roll out the dough to a rectangle 8 inches wide, and ¼ inch thick. Scatter the onion, bacon, parsley and shell fish all over it, and roll it up like a swiss roll. Seal the edge and the ends by pinching, and wrap in foil which has been well buttered. Boil in a covered oval casserole or baking dish with a lid, ⅓ full of water, on an upturned shallow dish, to keep it clear of the water. Check the water level every now and then, and boil for 2 hours. Remove carefully from the foil, keeping the juices. Add these to the juices in which the shell fish were originally opened. and serve with these offered separately, warmed, in a jug, and with another jug of melted butter, mixed with pepper, chopped parsley and chives.

Rabbit Pudding

1 jointed rabbit
1 lb. suet crust (made as above)
1 large onion
1 dstsp. sage
4 oz. mushrooms
4 oz. trimmed streaky bacon in one piece
Salt and black pepper

Soak the rabbit in salted water for 2 hours. Dry with a cloth. Line a greased pudding basin with ⅔ of the suet crust, rolled out to ¼ inch. Fill the crust with rabbit, onion rings, sliced mushroom, sage and strips of bacon, building up in layers, and sprinkling each layer with wholewheat flour, salt and pepper. Three quarters cover with water, and finish off with the remaining suet crust as a lid. Seal the rim with water, and trim. Top with greaseproof paper, and a pudding cloth, or foil. Boil in a large saucepan, ⅔ full of water for 3 hours, topping up with water as necessary. Turn out and slice at the table. serve with jacket potatoes, and root vegetables. No need for a sauce. Plenty of good sauce will ooze out when you cut the pudding.

You can make a similar pudding out of **steak and kidney, mixed game and pork and apple.**

Dishes Based on Batter

There are endless varieties on the theme of pancakes and fritters, relying on a batter. The quality and freshness of your flour is what makes or marrs it. The French prefer wholemeal flour for crêpes, and the large contingent from Normandy who visit our village every year for the annual twinning queue up in our mill for a bag of flour, freshly ground, to take home. It is worth investing in a 'tuile', or heavy French pancake griddle. You can buy really big ones from Brittany which are electrically heated, but I bought a simple one in Caen under the watchful eye of my French hostess, an excellent cook, and the champion rice pudding maker of Normandy.

Tuna Pancakes

For 2 or 4 (according to whether people come back for seconds)

4 oz. wholemeal flour
1 dstsp. sea salt
2 eggs
1 pt. milk
1 oz. sunflower or sesame seeds
1 oz. margarine
4 oz. tin of tuna in brine
1 tblsp. wholewheat flour
4 oz. grated cheddar cheese
1 tsp. mustard
2 hard-boiled eggs
Salt and pepper
Fennel or dill

Weigh the flour into a pudding basin, with the salt. Make a well in the centre, and break in the two eggs. Mix with a metal spoon, gradually drawing the flour into the eggs, adding milk as well, until you have a thin batter, about the consistency of cream. Beat with an egg beater, or in a mixer or liquidizer, and leave to stand for at least half an hour to allow the starch in the flour to swell. Make a sauce by melting margarine, adding a tablespoon of flour, stirring well, and then gradually adding milk to make a very stiff sauce. Add grated cheese and mustard, salt and pepper and some fennel or dill. Bring to the boil and cook for 3-4 minutes. Tip in the drained tuna, cut into large dice, and the sliced hard-boiled eggs. Heat your tuile, or heavy frying pan with a dessert spoon of oil, spread over the whole surface. Beat the batter mixture again, and add a little milk if it seems much thicker. Mix in the sesame or sunflower seeds. Pour 2 tablespoons of the batter onto the hot pan, and tip it and spread it with a spatula so that it covers most of the surface. The hotter the pan is, the crispier will be your pancakes.

When there are no liquid patches in the surface shake the pancake to free any points where it is sticking, then turn, either by tossing, or by flicking over with a metal spatula. Cook for moments only on the second side. Put onto a warm plate, and continue making pancakes, keeping them hot in a warm oven. You can pile them up, and put a large spoonful of filling in just before serving. This quantity makes 4 pancakes.

Yorkshire Pudding

Although Yorkshire pudding can not be called a main course, it is such an integral part of Sunday lunch, served with roast beef, that I am putting it in here, together with its less well-known cousin, *Marigold Pudding,* eaten with pork.

4 oz. plain unbleached white flour	*½ tsp. salt*
2 small eggs	*½ pt. milk*

Sift the flour into a bowl. Make a well in the middle, and mix as for pancake batter above, until all the milk is incorporated. Heat a pie dish or individual shallow dishes in a hot oven (425), with enough dripping to make a thin layer over the bottom when melted. Wait until the dish/es are very hot, and pour in the batter, having added a tablespoon of cold water. Cook for 20 minutes for a large pudding, or 10 minutes for small ones. Look at them then, and see if they are puffy and have risen. If not, leave for a little longer.

Marigold Pudding
Is made the same way, but a little chopped sage and a handful of common marigold petals are added to the batter when it is made. This makes a delicious flavoured golden pudding, with a peppery flavour, to eat with pork. An old English idea.

Elvers with Bread and Butter

Catch the elvers in March in a small bucket in many of the streams and rivers, specially in the South West. Tip them into an old pillow case, take them home, and rinse them well, still in the pillowcase, under a running tap. Pick out any debris. Wrap a towel round the pillowcase, and gently press dry.

1 lb. elvers	*Large clove of garlic, crushed*
4 oz. diced fat bacon	*2 tblsps. chopped parsley*
2 tblsps. olive oil	*Salt and pepper*
Juice of a lemon	*Half an onion, finely chopped*

Fry the bacon in a heavy pan, until it is crisp and brown, and until the fat runs. Add the olive oil, garlic, onion and half the parsley. Increase the heat and put in the elvers with a pierced spoon making sure they are properly drained. Stir for a few seconds until they turn white. Remove, and serve hot with salt, pepper and the rest of the parsley, and a squeeze of lemon juice. Hand a plate of freshly cut wholewheat bread and butter with them.

Peg's Fish Pie

My Aunt Peg, in her fish pie, uses breadcrumbs instead of potatoes. This is a great favourite with all our family.

1 lb. cod fillet, poached in milk, or fish stock, with fennel and a bay leaf, seasoned with salt and pepper
12 oz. white breadcrumbs
8 oz. grated cheese
1 oz. butter
1 oz. flour
½ pt. of the milk used for poaching the fish or mixed milk and fish stock
¼ lb. mushrooms, lightly sautéed
2 hard-boiled eggs, sliced, or a few prawns

Skin the poached fish, and use the liquid to make a cheese sauce. First melt the butter, and then add the flour, stirring well, and then, gradually, the poaching liquid and half the grated cheese. Simmer until you have a fairly thick sauce. Season with salt and pepper. Grease a dish, and line with a cupful of the breadcrumbs. Sprinkle on a layer of the grated cheese, then a layer of flaked fish with a few of the mushrooms added to it. Continue like this until the dish is three quarters full. Finish with a fish layer, and top with hard boiled egg or prawns. Pour cheese sauce over it, and bake in a moderate oven for forty minutes, or until it is brown on top.

Dough-based Meals

Pizzas have become one of our most common convenience foods, and there are several methods of making the dough. In both these variations, wholewheat flour is used, which fits in well with the rough, country taste of the true pizza, traditionally a working man's lunch in Italy.

Yeast-dough Pizza

8 oz. wholewheat flour
1 tsp. salt
1 tsp. sugar
½ oz. yeast
12 oz. tinned Italian tomatoes
1 lb. sliced onions
6 oz. chedder cheese (or belpaese)
1 tblsp. basil
½ pt. warm milk
2 small eggs
½ oz. butter
10 anchovy fillets
16 plumb black olives
3 tblsps. olive oil
Salt and black pepper

Warm the flour and salt in a bowl. Cream the yeast with the warm milk, with specks of butter in it. Add the beaten eggs, and warm a little again to blood heat. Add to the flour and put it in a warm place to rise for half an hour. Meanwhile, soften the onion in oil, on low heat. Knead the dough on a floured board, and spread out by hand onto a greased and floured pizza tin, into a large round, about 10 inches. Leave to rise for ten minutes more. Drain the onions, and spread on the dough. Cut the tomatoes in half and spread on the onions, not using too much juice. Sprinkle grated cheese all over it. Season with salt, pepper and basil. Decorate the top with strip of anchovy, in a lattice, and put an olive in each square you form. You can use **bacon and mushroom topping instead, or tuna and caper.** The permutations are endless.

Lastly, here is my favourite recipe, invented to make use of the many times my fisherman husband comes home with *one* beautiful trout, and I have to think how to make a meal for two out of it.

Trout Soufflée

1 brown trout, of about half a pound
2 oz. onion sliced
A bay leaf
Sea salt and pepper
3/4 pt. mixed white wine and water (or water with 1 tsp. wine vinegar in it)
1½ oz. butter
1 heaped tblsp. wholewheat flour
1/4 pt. milk
1/4 lb. grated cheese (cheddar)
4 eggs
Parsley and thyme

Poach the trout with onion, bay leaf, salt and pepper, wine and water, parsley and thyme. Cook for only about a minute on each side, in gently simmering liquid. Allow to cool, while you make the soufflée mixture. Oil a soufflée dish six or seven inches in diameter. Melt the butter in a large saucepan, stir in the flour, mixing well and add some of the strained liquid you poached the fish in, and the milk. Bring to the boil and mix in the grated cheese, so that you have a thick sauce. Adjust the seasoning. Flake the fish, and put the pieces in the bottom of the soufflée dish, being careful to fillet it first, so that you do not include any bones. When the sauce has cooled a little, add the egg yolks, breaking the whites into a pudding basin. Beat the whites to a stiff peak, and fold into the rest of the mixture with a metal spoon. Pour into the soufflée dish, and cook at 375 degrees for 35 minutes.

Muncaster
Mill
Cumbria

Mapledurham Mill Wholewheat Pizza

Mildred Cookson, at Mapledurham Mill in Oxfordshire makes wholewheat flour, and brown and unbleached white flour.

Base
8 oz. wholewheat flour
1½ oz. margarine
2 tsp. baking powder
1 tsp. salt
4 tblsps. milk

Topping
12 oz. can tomatoes
1 large onion
1 small pepper
1 tblsp. oil
Mixed herbs
Bay leaf
Slice ham/bacon
Grated cheese
Flour for thickening

Rub margarine into dry ingredients. Gradually add beaten egg and mix together with a wooden spoon. Add enough milk to make a workable dough. Turn out onto a floured board. Knead well for 5 minutes and roll out to required size. Place on a greased baking sheet and bake at 400 degrees or gas mark 6 for 10 minutes, until base becomes firm to touch. Gently fry chopped onion in oil Add tomatoes and simmer. To thicken, add about 1 tblsp. of flour stirring all the time. Add some grated cheese, seasoning and mixed herbs. Leave to cool. Cover partly cooked base with topping and decorate with rings of pepper, chopped bacon or ham, grated cheese and bay leaf. Bake at 400 degrees/gas mark 6 for a further 20 minutes.

Mapledurham Watermill, Nr. Reading, Oxon. The last working watermill on the Thames still producing flour.

3. Vegetarian and Vegan Cooking

Vegetarian and vegan cookery has become integrated into our lives in the past decade. People are much more conscious than they were that we are putting a great burden onto the world's resources by continuing to produce livestock, which need large tracts of land to feed them, a luxurious way of feeding ourselves in the developed northern hemisphere, while part of the southern hemisphere is radically short of food. Although the majority of us still enjoy meat and fish at least some of the time, a growing minority, particularly of young people, are vegetarians through a conviction that only this way, little by little, can we solve the world's food problems. Traditional millers are, many of us, concerned too with the pressure on world resources by the over-use of non-renewable energy in the form of oil and coal. Although we can none of us claim to be filling the energy gap by using the power of wind and water in this country, the strong interest by the many people who come to our mills in the practical use of these old technologies to produce excellent basic foodstuffs, is to many of us very encouraging. The use of intermediate technology in developing countries, too, is only possible by the old techniques being remembered, and practised where they have been of use for over a thousand years.

At least as strong an incentive to eat vegetarian and vegan foods as consciousness of the world's food and energy problems is the instinct many of us have towards a healthy diet, as free from additives as possible. Intensive farming relies heavily on the use of chemicals and anti-biotics, which leach into the rivers and the sea, adding to the industrial pollutants also there. Convenience foods and even such basics as mass-produced flours and cereals contain additives, and long-distance distribution means that even vegetables and fruit tend to be sprayed with preservatives to prolong their shelf life. Although it is probably impossible to protect oneself completely from synthetic ingredients, (and many would argue that trying to do so would be carrying interest in one's own well-being to extremes) there are many simple ways of improving the quality of one's diet. The vegetarian and vegan revolution has certainly helped, together with the interest in organically grown cereal crops, still only in its infancy in most countries, but treated very seriously by many traditional millers.

What used to be thought of as limitations in vegetarian cookery, variety and taste, have now been overcome by the introduction of flavours and dishes from many countries. My vegetarian aunt Ann, who walked in the fells until a year before her death at ninety three, was lucky to have a daughter-in-law who was Spanish, and another who was Indian, as the two cuisines introduced different elements into her already delicious cookery. There are many ways of keeping the flavour in vegetable dishes, whether they are wholewheat pastries or pittas, homemade pastas or pancakes, pizzas, breadcrumb toppings or cornmeal tortillas.

The letter 'V' before a recipe indicates that it is vegan.

Courgette Quiche

¾ lb. wholewheat puff pastry (see p. 19)
6 eggs
½ pt. thick natural yoghurt
½ pt. milk
4 oz. grated cheddar cheese
1 lb. courgettes
1 tsp. basil
Sea salt, and freshly ground black pepper

Roll out the pastry as thin as possible and line a 9 inch flan tin, well greased. Weigh down with a round of greaseproof paper, and dry beans, and bake at 400 degrees for 10 minutes. Take from the oven and remove beans and paper. Mix the milk, yoghurt, eggs, salt and pepper in a liquidizer. Liquidize well. Pour into the pastry case, and top with sliced courgettes, grated cheese and basil, brushing the courgette slices with a little oil. Bake at 375 degrees for 35-40 minutes.

You can make the same quiche with **tomato and chopped chives, and mushroom** (For this, slice half a pound of mushrooms so that they keep their outline, and simmer for 4 minutes with seasoning, before topping the quiche with them).

'V' Spinach Quiche

¾ lb. wholewheat puff pastry (see p. 19)
½ lb. tofu (bean curd)
½ pt. soya milk
1 tsp. sea salt
4 oz. walnuts
1 tblsp. sunflower oil
1 oz. vegetable margarine
1 tblsp. wholewheat flour
1 tsp. bicarbonate of soda
1 tsp. cream of tartar
1 tsp. freshly ground black pepper
1 lb. spinach, boiled with salt, in
1 tblsp. water

Roll out the pastry and bake 'blind' as above, in a 9 inch flan tin. Fry the walnuts and half the tofu, in cubes, in sunflower oil until they are crisp. Drain the cooked spinach and chop finely. Melt the margarine, mix in the flour, and add soya milk slowly to make a thick sauce. Season with salt and pepper. Pour into a liquidizer, add half the tofu, cut into small cubes and the bicarbonate of soda and cream of tartar. Liquidize well. Line the flan case with the spinach, pour the sauce on top, and scatter the walnuts and tofu on top. Bake at 375 degrees for 35-40 minutes. Alternative fillings for this quiche are **'V' cauliflower and pine nuts, 'V' sprouts and hazelnut and 'V' peanut and sweetcorn.**

Otterton Mill Vegetarian Pasties

We make these pasties, and the vegan curry pasties that follow at our bakery at Otterton Mill. Ian, the baker, is tall, and I always think this is an advantage for rolling out pastry, nice and quick. You can get right above it. We sell these pasties, too, in Exeter, in the market, on Thursdays and they are available at the Bran Tub, an excellent health food shop in the Magdalene Road.

For 12 pasties
1 lb. wholewheat puff pastry (see p. 19)
2 medium sized onions
2 carrots
Beaten egg
3 oz. swede or parsnip
1 medium sized potato
6 oz. cheddar cheese
1 tsp. chopped thyme
1 dstsp. sea salt
Freshly ground black pepper

Roll out the pastry, and cut rounds the size of a tea plate. Grate all the vegetables, and the cheese. Mix with the seasoning and thyme, and put a dollop into the centre of each piece of pastry. Wet the edges with water and seal together into a half-circle, crimping the top. Brush with beaten egg, and cook on greased baking sheets, at 450 degrees, for 15 minutes. Cool on wire trays.

'V' Curry Pasties

For 12 pasties

1 lb. wholewheat puff pastry (see p. 19)
1½ lb. vegetables, quite finely diced (leeks, potatoes, carrots, onions, swede, parsnip, etc).
2 apples, cut into small pieces
4 heaped tsps. curry powder
2 tblsps. tomato purée
1 tsp. honey
3 tblsps. vegetable oil
1 tsp. sea salt
Black pepper
1 tblsp. wholewheat flour
¼ pt. water (approx)

Fry the vegetables and apples with the curry powder for a few minutes, then add the tomato purée, honey, salt and pepper and water. Simmer until tender, with a lid on the pan. Allow to cool. Roll out the pastry, and cut into rounds the size of a tea plate. Place a dollop of the mixture in each round. Wet the edges with water, and draw up into a half circle, sealing along the top. Bake at 425 degrees for 15-20 minutes. Cool on a wire tray.

Otterton Mill, Nr. Budleigh Salterton, Devon.
The River Otter powers this Domesday mill.

Homemade Pasta

For this you need strong white flour, strong wholewheat, or finest semolina. Most people do not succeed immediately in making fresh pasta, but it is worth persevering, as there are few more delicious ways of using flour than in some of the myriad pasta-based dishes. Of course, many of them are not vegetarian, but for vegetarian cookery fresh pasta does add a dimension to the flavour, and also protein in the form of the eggs which are used in the making.

1½ lb. flour (as above)
A pinch of salt
6 eggs

Sift the flour onto a floured surface with the salt. Make a well in the centre, and break the eggs in one at a time, drawing the flour and eggs together with your fingers, so that the liquid does not escape. Gradually mix into a dough, then knead with the base of both hands, putting your weight behind it. Continue for 15 minutes. Divide the dough into four. Roll out each lump on a floured surface until it is wafer thin, and rectangular in shape. This will be difficult at first, but suddenly the dough will 'give' and become drier, and more manageable. Dry each sheet on a cloth, draped over a chair. If you get interested in making fresh pasta, invest in a pasta making machine, which will cut noodles to the width you want. Ravioli can be made easily by rolling out a sheet of pasta, putting small blobs of filling at spaced intervals on it, and topping with another sheet, after wetting with beaten egg, and then cutting out with a pastry cutter. Lasagne can also be made easily, by cutting sheets to the areas of your dish.

Vegetarian Lasagne

1½ oz. vegetable margarine
2 heaped tblsps. wholewheat flour
1 tblsp. tomato purée
1 cup soya mince, simmered for 4 minutes in 1½ cups water, with a little oil
½ lb. mozzarella cheese
2 oz. parmesan cheese
3-4 sheets of lasagne, made as above
1 pt. milk
2 onions
2 cloves garlic
1 tblsp. olive oil
Sea salt and pepper
2 tblsps. parsley

Make a white sauce by melting the margarine, adding the flour and gradually adding the milk. Bring to the boil and simmer for a few minutes until it is thick. Season, and put on one side. Make another sauce by cooking the onions gently in oil, then adding the garlic and tomato purée, and the soya mince. Cook gently for 15 minutes or so. Put a layer of mince sauce in a rectangular dish, then a layer of white sauce, a sprinkling of cheese and parsley, then a layer of lasagne. Continue until all the ingredients are used up, finishing with cheese. Pour over half a tin of tomatoes, liquidized with seasoning. Do not completely submerge the top layers. Bake at 375 degrees for 40 minutes, until golden brown on top.

Vegan Lasagne

Many proprietary brands of pasta are not made with egg. For a vegan variation, use the same recipe, substituting lasagne verde, soya milk, and for the cheese layer, minced tofu flavoured with marmite. Chopped nuts on top will make a crisp crust. A very nourishing meal, containing plenty of protein.

Mushroom Pizza

Follow the recipe on p. 29, but for anchovy topping substitute mushrooms, sliced to keep their profiles, simmered for a few minutes in 2 tblsps. water. Brush them with oil before baking the pizza, and make a pretty pattern with them on top of the pizza. Alternatively, use **sliced courgettes or olives.**

Vegetarian and Vegan Fillings for Pitta Bread and Cornbread

Pitta bread (see p. 13) can be filled with endless varieties of fillings. For a vegan equivalent, make cornbread, and use it in the same way.

'V' Cornmeal Tortillas

1 lb. cornmeal
1 tsp. baking powder
½ pt. warm water and soya milk, mixed
1 tsp. sea salt

Sift the cornmeal, baking powder and salt in to a bowl. Gradually add the liquid, and mix to a soft dough. Roll out to three quarters of an inch, and cut into circles about 5 inches in diameter. Bake at 400 degrees for 20 30 minutes, until golden brown. You can add 2 oz. sesame seeds to the mixture for a crispy bite.

Fillings

Lentil Paste

Made with 1 lb. lentils, boiled with water, drained, and liquidized with ¼ sliced onion and 4 oz. grated cheese, salt and pepper, while the lentils are still hot. Mix with toasted sunflower seeds, and 2 tblsps. natural yoghurt, 1 tblsp. oil.

'V' Eggplant Paté

Bake an eggplant in the oven in an oiled dish for 30 minutes. Remove, and peel the skin off. Chop into a liquidizer with a quarter of an onion, chopped, a clove of garlic, 1 tblsp. cider vinegar, 2 tblsp. olive oil, salt and pepper. Liquidize thoroughly, and put in the fridge. Mix with pine nuts, diced cucumber, and shredded lettuce.

'V' Marinated Tofu with Salad

Make a marinade from ½ tsp. soya sauce, a pinch of cayenne pepper, ½ tsp. crushed cumin seeds, ½ tsp. crushed coriander seeds, 1 tsp. sea salt, a bay leaf, 6 tblsps. sesame oil (or sunflower oil), 6 tblsps. white wine vinegar. Marinate the tofu in it overnight. Chop 2 tomatoes finely, and mix with the drained tofu and 1 oz. toasted sesame seeds.

Vegetarian Sausage Meat

Most of the proprietary brands of vegetarian sausage meat are so revolting, it is worth making up your own.

2 cups soya mince, beef flavour
3 cups water
1 tblsp. olive oil
1 medium onion, finely chopped
½ cup wholewheat breadcrumbs
1 tblsp. chopped parsley
Sea salt and pepper
1 egg

Simmer the soya mince in water, with the oil, for 4 minutes. Drain off any excess water. Put into a bowl with the rest of the ingredients mixing well.

Vegetarian Scotch Eggs

For 4 Scotch eggs:
The above quantity of sausage meat
4 hard-boiled eggs
Wholewheat seasoned flour
1 egg, lightly beaten
4 oz. wholewheat breadcrumbs
Oil for deep frying

Shell the hard-boiled eggs, and roll in seasoned flour. Divide the sausage meat into four, and flatten each piece into a square on a floured board. Put each hard-boiled egg in the middle of a square, and shape the sausage meat round it. Coat in beaten egg and breadcrumbs and deep fry for about 5 minutes.

Boardhouse Mill Beremeal Pancakes

Fergus Morrison at Boardhouse Mill, Orkney, is the only producer of Beremeal, a kind of barley with a unique flavour which has been grown on Orkney for at least two thousand years. It can be bought by mail order from the mill.

4 oz. Beremeal
3 eggs
1 oz. melted butter
Water to mix

Sift the flour into a bowl, make a well in the centre and add eggs and butter; mix with water until smooth. Beat well. Leave to rest. Pour onto a moderately hot, lightly greased girdle in ladlefuls, slightly tilting to spread the mixture. Cook for two minutes on each side. Place filling in centre, fold in four, and eat hot.

Parsnip and Carrot Batter Pudding

4 oz. unbleached white flour
1 level tsp. baking powder
3 eggs
½ pt. milk
Sea salt and black pepper
2 tblsps. nut oil or sesame oil
1 medium onion
4 oz. diced carrot
4 oz. diced parsnip
1 dstsp. thyme
1 dstsp. curry powder

Sift the flour and baking powder into a large bowl. Make a well in the centre and break the eggs in one at a time, gradually drawing the flour into the liquid. Continue mixing in the milk in the same way, and beat until you have a smooth creamy mixture. Season with salt and pepper, and put on one side. Put the oil in a baking dish in the oven. Roll the vegetables in curry powder, salt and pepper and thyme. Add to the baking dish, and cook, until they are tender, covered with a piece of foil. (25 minutes). Remove the foil, and put the baking dish further up in the oven to get very hot. When it is, beat the batter again and pour into the dish. Bake for 20 minutes at 400 degrees. You can make a batter pudding with other vegetables too, such as **aubergine or courgettes.** For both of these, use olive oil and orgegano, instead of nut oil and thyme.

Vegetarian Pancake Fillings

Use the pancake recipe on p. 27. You can add either sesame or sunflower seeds to the batter to give it crunch and more protein. Then try one of the fillings on the next page.

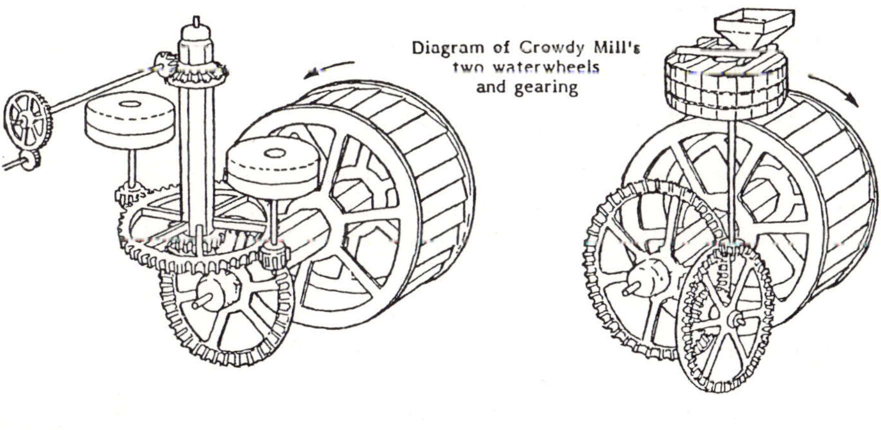

Crowdy Mill, Harbertonford, Devon.
Driven by two waterwheels, on the River Harbourne.

Cheese and Hard-Boiled Egg Filling

1 oz. vegetable margarine
1½ oz. wholewheat flour
¼ pt. milk
3 hard-boiled eggs
2 oz. chopped walnuts
1 tsp. chopped thyme
4 oz. grated cheddar
1 tsp. mustard powder
Sea salt and black pepper

Melt the margarine, add the flour, stirring well. Gradually add the milk and thyme, salt and pepper, still stirring. Bring to the boil and cook for a few minutes on a low heat until it is thick. Add the grated cheese and mustard, and keep on the heat for a little longer. Slice the hard-boiled eggs, and add to the sauce with the walnuts, lightly toasted in the oven. Cook the pancakes as on p. 27, and put a dollop of filling into each one.

Onion, Mushroom and Pine-Nut Filling

Half an onion
4 oz. mushrooms
A clove of garlic
1 oz. pine nuts
¼ pt. natural yoghurt (thick)
4 oz. cream cheese
Sea salt and black pepper
Half a green pepper
1 tblsp. olive oil

Fry the finely chopped onion in the oil, then add the finely chopped pepper, the pine-nuts and finally the mushrooms, with the crushed garlic clove. Mix the yoghurt and cream cheese together in a pan, heating gently, but not boiling. Add the fried ingredients, and mix well, seasoning with salt and pepper. Use to fill pancakes.

Courgette Fritters with a Sour Cream Sauce

1 lb. courgettes
¾ pt. sour cream or half and half yoghurt and cream
4 oz. wholewheat flour
1 large egg
⅛ pt. water
Oil for deep frying
1 clove of garlic, crushed with salt

Cook the courgettes whole in boiling water for 10 minutes, with 1 tsp. salt. Drain and cool. Mix together the flour with ½ tsp. salt and make a well in the middle. Beat the egg with the water, and pour this into the well. Mix thoroughly, and beat until the mixture is smooth. Add more water if it is too thick. It should be the consistency of double cream. Heat the oil. Cut the courgettes into medium thick rounds. Dip the rounds into the batter and fry in hot oil until they are golden brown. Drain on kitchen paper and keep warm. Beat the yoghurt or sour cream, and add salt and garlic. Spread over the fritters before serving.

'V' Vegetable Pudding

10 oz. wholewheat flour
1½ tsps. baking powder
½ tsp. sea salt
5 oz. hard vegetable margarine
3 sliced tomatoes
Seat salt and pepper
4 oz. chopped onion
4 oz. diced carrot
4 oz. diced parsnip
4 oz. sliced mushrooms
4 oz. diced tofu
1 dstsp. sage
1 tblsp. parsley
1 tblsp. sunflower oil

Mix flour, baking powder, salt and margarine together in a bowl, and add enough water to make a soft dough. Stand in a cool place. Prepare the vegetables. Roll out the dough and take three quarters of it to line a pudding basin, well greased. Fill with the vegetables, building up in layers, and including the sage and parsley, and the tofu. Pour in a tablespoonful of sunflower oil, season well with salt and pepper. Top with the rest of the crust, wetting the edges to get a good seal. Cover with a cloth, tied on with string. Boil for 2 hours in a pan half full of water, topping it up as necessary.

Vegetable Curry with Parathas

Many parts of India have large vegetarian populations, and traditional cookery which goes back hundreds of years. Parathas are griddle cakes from the Punjab, and they are an excellent accompaniment to this vegetable curry, which has a vegan variation.

2 lb. vegetables, for example French beans, peas, potatoes, carrots and cauliflower
2 chopped onions
6 oz. desiccated coconut
½ tsp. garam masala, made from 1 cinnamon stick, 1 clove and 1 peppercorn, freshly ground
½ pt. water
10 red chillies
1 oz. poppy seeds
½ tsp. turmeric
1 tblsp. fresh ginger, grated
2 oz. vegetable oil
½ pt. natural yoghurt
¼ pt. single cream
1 tsp. honey
Salt to taste
2 cloves garlic

Boil the vegetables separately, in a little water, except for the 2 potatoes which should be boiled gently, *covered* with water, until cooked. Dice them when you have drained them, divide the cauliflower into florets, and slice the beans and carrots. Grind the onions, coconut, chillies, poppy seeds, garlic, turmeric and ginger to a paste. Melt the oil in a heavy based saucepan, add the curry paste and cook for a few minutes. Stir in the garam masala and then the vegetables and water. Bring to the boil and cook uncovered, for a few minutes more. Stir in the yoghurt, cream, honey and salt. Serve hot with parathas.

Parathas

1 lb. wholewheat flour
½ tsp. salt
4 oz. vegetable oil
12 fl. oz. water

Sift the flour into a bowl with salt. Rub in half the oil and mix with water to make a soft dough. Shape into balls, about 12, and roll out into flat circles, about 6 inches in diameter. Fold in half and then into quarters, and roll out again. Do this several times, each time you fold the parathas, brushing them with melted oil. Cook on a hot griddle or heavy frying pan for a minute. Brush oil round the edges, and turn. Remove when they are brown on both sides.

'V' for a vegan variation, substitute ½ pt. soya milk and 4 oz. tofu, liquidized together, for the yoghurt and cream.

Red Cabbage and Nut Strudel

1 large red cabbage
¼ pt. water
1 tsp. dill seeds
1 tblsp. cider vinegar
1 tsp. sea salt
4 oz. roasted hazel nuts, roughly chopped
½ lb. unbleached white flour
1 egg
1 tblsp. sunflower oil
½ tsp. sea salt
A little water

Slice the red cabbage into strips. Put into the ¼ pt. of water, boiling and seasoned with sea salt and dill seeds. Boil for 5 minutes, so that it is still just crisp. Drain off the water. (Keep for making soup.) Stir in the cider vinegar. Leave to cool while you make the strudel dough. Tip the flour in a heap onto a large board, and make a well in the middle. Break the egg in, and oil and salt. Mix with a knife, adding a little water, then knead with your hands to form a soft dough. To begin with, the dough will be sticky, but persevere, and in about 15 minutes the dough will have bubbles in it, and be elastic and manageable. Flour your board again, cover the dough with a basin, and leave for an hour. Roast the hazelnuts for 10 minutes in a hot oven, and give them a few seconds in a coffee grinder, or chop roughly. Roll out the dough to the size of your large board, then transfer to a floured cloth, about the size of a small table cloth (a piece of sheeting will do). Pull and stretch the dough until it is paper thin. Scatter the cabbage and nuts all over it, and roll it up, after trimming the edges. Slide onto an oiled baking sheet, brush with oil, and bake at 375 degrees for 30 minutes.

4. Puddings and Desserts

We do not eat puddings like we used to. Probably our health is better for it, but it is noticeable that one of our national dishes is Christmas Pudding, which we eat with relish once a year, as if to defy the ban on stodgey eating that went out with the suet pudding. Even in 1692 Thomas Tryon was warning against eating too much pudding. Here is what he had to say.

Of the best sort of Puddens, and the Contrary

> This is a great sort of Food in England, we are famous for it abroad, and there is no Nation besides, that I have known or heard of, that practises it so much ... Such foods ought not to be eaten by any that love their Health and Strength. For common sense may suggest what a strange, disorderly jumble and Mishmash so many contrary ingredients must make when boil'd together in the Stomach.

A few of our old favourites have survived, however, and many of them are based on the filling recipes of the past, with sweet pastries and batters coming into their own in seasonal puddings like Shrove Tuesday pancakes, and Christmas mince pies. The all-year-round trifle uses flour-based sponge cake, and summer pudding relies on slices of bread to hold it together. Good freshly-ground flour can only add to the flavour of puddings. Several mills have their own Christmas recipes, and here, too, are recipes for babas and cheesecakes, flummery and open tarts, and even the old English brown bread ice, brought up to date with carob and mint. Probably Thomas Tryon would disapprove of this too!

Maud Foster Mill Christmas Pudding

Tom, James and Ruby Waterfield have restored this, the tallest working windmill in England in the centre of Boston, Lincs. They make wholewheat 85% brown, white unbleached flours, a rye flour, pancake flour, buckwheat flour, wheat flakes, oat flakes, semolina and bran.

½ lb. raisins
¾ lb. sultanas
½ lb. currants
½ lb. chopped peel
3 oz. chopped almonds
8 oz. wholemeal flour
6 oz. breadcrumbs
½ tsp. mixed spice
12 oz. shredded suet
1 lb. soft brown sugar
4 eggs
¼ pt. to ½ pt. water
Juice and grated rind of 1 lemon
1 grated carrot

Mix flour, breadcrumbs, spice, suet, fruit, almonds, sugar and grated carrot. Beat the eggs and add ¼ pt. water, then stir into the mixture. Add more water if required to make a stiff dough. Add lemon juice then stir again. Fill 2 well greased pudding basins with the mixture and cover with aluminium foil. Steam for about 6 hours. Cook for another hour before serving. It will sometimes be convenient to steam the puddings in the oven by the timer. Cover the basins with aluminium foil, and stand inside a larger basin, on a pastry cutter. Half fill this second basin with water, and seal with aluminium foil. Cook in the oven for 6 hours at 350 degrees, overnight if it suits you.

P.S. Get the family to have a stir and a wish – it's an easy way to mix well.

(Vegetarian puddings may be made by substituting vegetable margarine for suet).

Maud Foster Mill, Boston, Lincs. This mill has 7 floors and stands 80 feet high. It trims itself to wind with a fantail and there are 5 self regulating sails.

Open Fruit Tarts

The sweet pastry for these colourful fruit tarts may be made with wholewheat flour, which gives it a nutty, crisp consistency.

6 oz. wholewheat flour
4 oz. butter (preferably)
1 egg
3 tblsps. sugar
A pinch of salt
2 lb. fruit, either 1½ lb. raspberries and ½ lb. red currants, or pears or plums
1 tblsp. redcurrant or apple jelly

Mix the dry ingredients in a bowl, and rub in the butter with your fingertips, keeping it cool. Mix in the beaten egg quickly. Tip into a greased 9 inch flan case and push it with your fingers to line the case evenly, drawing it up to the sides, and cutting off neatly at the top. Fill with beans and bake at 350 degrees for 15 minutes. Be careful it does not burn. Take it out of the oven, and allow to cool. Put the fruit into a pan with 6 oz. white sugar, and simmer for a few minutes, not long enough for it to lose its shape. Fill the cooled pastry with the drained fruit, arranging pears or plums in a pattern face downward. Put back into the oven for ten minutes. To the juice of the fruit, add the jelly, and cook quickly until it forms a thick syrup. Pour it over the fruit when it has cooled.

For **apple tart**, leave the sugar out of the pastry recipe, and arrange finely sliced apples on it with 4 oz. sugar between the layers. Bake all together, without baking the pastry first, for 30-40 minutes.

Otterton Mill Mince Pies

1¼ lb. currants
1¼ lb. sultanas
1 lb. raisins
¾ lb. mixed peel
6 large Bramley seedlings, cored, peeled and chopped
¼ lb. shredded almonds
The rind of a lemon
The juice of 2 lemons
¾ lb. soft brown sugar
1 tsp. sea salt
6 bananas
¼ lb. glacé cherries
½ lb. melted margarine
Light ale
½ tsp. ground cloves
1 tsp. allspice
1 tsp. cinnamon
1 tsp. freshly grated nutmeg
Wholemeal puff pastry

Mix all the ingredients in the order given. This quantity of mincemeat will keep for 2-3 weeks, and you can keep it in a covered jar, and use it when you want.

For 2 dozen mince pies, use 1½ lb. wholemeal puff pastry (see p. 19).

Flummery

This is an adaptation of an old Welsh dessert, and, unusually, makes use of semolina. Several traditional mills produce this, and it is the result of a fine separation of flour and bran, leaving wheat granules of varying fineness, connected in some people's minds with the dull milk puddings of childhood. This dessert does not come into that category and is suitable for a lunch party.

2 oz. semolina
½ pt. water
2 glasses sweet white wine
A squeeze of lemon juice
1 oz. castor sugar
The whites of 2 eggs
Puréed fruit, mixed with a little sugar
¼ pt. double cream

Pour the wine and water into a pan, with the squeeze of lemon juice. Bring to the boil, stir in the semolina and simmer for 5 minutes until it is cooked. Stir frequently to prevent it from sticking. Draw it aside and stir in the sugar. Allow it to cool, and if it is thicker than dropping consistency, add a little more water. When it is quite cool, whip the cream and fold into the mixture, and finally the well beaten egg whites. Turn into glasses. Serve with a fresh fruit purée. Raspberries or strawberries are most suitable. (Frozen fruit will do.)

Frumenty

This, on the other hand, is an old English dessert, whose name derives from the Latin frumentum, or corn. Not a party dish, it is more a comforting meal for anyone who is ill. This recipe comes from an early nineteenth century hand-written 'Receipt Book'.

> 1 pt. new milk, leaving out ¼ pint for mixing the flour with – ½ pint of *creed wheat* (see below). Put these into a good sized brass or iron pan with a pinch of salt, mix one good dessertspoonful of flour into a smooth paste with ¼ pint of milk. Put it into the pan just before boiling, stirring it carefully all the time to prevent its setting when it boils. Put in 2 oz. sultana raisins and ¼ pint currants. Sweeten to your taste (takes about 1 tablespoonful). When it has boiled 10 minutes put in the spices – half a small teaspoonful of allspice and a pinch of powdered cinnamon – and let the whole boil for 5 or 6 minutes longer or till there is no taste of flour.

Creed Wheat is wheat, boiled in water to soften it. It needs about half an hour, and organically grown wheat should be used. Don't bother about a brass or iron pan, of course.

Ginger Cheesecake

Pastry made as for Open Fruit Tart
3/4 lb. fresh cream cheese
2 eggs
2 tsps. lemon juice
1 oz. freshly grated root ginger
1/2 lb. cream, soured with lemon juice
1/2 lb. castor sugar
2 oz. chrystallized ginger

Blind bake the pastry in a 9 inch flan case. Mix the cheese, half the sugar, eggs, lemon juice and grated ginger in a blender. Blend very well. Tip into the pastry lining, and bake at 350 degrees for 20 minutes. Mix the soured cream with the rest of the sugar and the chrystallized ginger. Spread over the cheesecake while it is still hot, and return to the oven for a few minutes. Chill well before serving.

Sussex Pond Pudding

This is a really wicked pudding, full of ingredients which are bad for you. It is probably only defensible if made for a large hungry, growing family. It is delicious, though.

8 oz. wholewheat flour
1 1/2 tsps. baking powder
4 oz. fresh suet
4 oz. butter
1/4 pt. milk and water, mixed
1 large lemon
4 oz. demerara sugar

Make a suet crust, mixing the flour, baking powder, salt, suet and milk and water in a mixing bowl until you have a soft dough. Roll it out on a floured board, and use 3/4 of it to line a well greased pudding basin. Put in half the sugar and butter, then the lemon, standing upright in the middle. Top up with the rest of the sugar and butter, and make a lid with the rest of the dough. Seal with water round the edges. Cover with a cloth, and boil for 3 hours. Turn out, and cut, giving everyone a piece of lemon.

Summer Pudding

1 1/2 lb. blackberries and
2 large cooking apples or
1 1/2 lb. raspberries, with or without 1/2 lb. red currants (If you are not using red currants, increase the quantity of raspberries).
1/4 lb. sugar
A stale tin loaf, either white or wholemeal

Stew the fruit with sugar for 5 minutes or so, until the juices run. Line a greased pudding basin with slices of stale bread, cut thin (about 1/4 inch). Make sure there are no gaps. Tip in half the fruit, without the juice, and half way up the pudding put in another layer of bread, lying flat. Fill up with the rest of the fruit. Tip in a little juice, so that there is enough to seep into the bread and colour it, but no so much that it becomes a sloppy mess which will not stand up. Top with a lid of bread slices. (Remove the crusts, of course, of all the bread slices before you start.) Put a saucer or plate onto the pudding, and a heavy weight of about three or four pounds. Leave until the following day. Turn out onto a dish, sprinkle with sugar, and serve with thin cream.

Brown Bread Ice with Carob and Mint Sauce

2 eggs
2 yolks of egg
2 oz. sugar
½ pt. milk
Vanilla essence
½ pt. lightly whipped cream
3 tblsps. brown breadcrumbs
1 tblsp. castor sugar
3 oz. carob bar
Peppermint essence
1 tsp. carob powder

Beat the eggs and sugar together in a blender. Pour on the warm milk, and turn into a double saucepan. Heat gently, stirring until it is thick and custard-like. Add vanilla essence, and allow to cool. When it is cool, fold in the lightly whipped cream. Put in the freezer until it is partly frozen, then remove and beat. Turn into a plastic container, and continue freezing. Meanwhile, put the breadcrumbs with the castor sugar into a moderate oven, on a baking sheet until they are brown. Allow to cool, and stir into the ice cream. Return to the freezer. To make the sauce: break the carob bar into a saucepan with carob powder and ¼ pt. water. Stir over a moderate heat until it is boiling. Add ¼ pt. more water, and ½ tsp. peppermint essence. Simmer for 15 minutes until it is thick. Remove from the heat and cool a little. Put a little of the sauce into a cup, and mix well with an egg yolk. Return to the rest of the sauce, and stir until it is thick. Serve the ice cream with sauce poured over each portion.

Gooseberry Charlotte

A loaf of white bread
1½ lb. of gooseberries
4 oz. sugar
1 head of elderflower
4 tblsps. water
4 oz. butter
Single cream

Slice the bread into ¼ inch slices, cutting off the crusts. Stew the gooseberries with water, sugar and elderflower for 20 minutes, over a gentle heat. Remove the elderflower, and purée the gooseberries in a liquidizer. Line a charlotte mould with slices of bread, dipped in melted butter. Pour in the fruit purée and cover with more bread, also dipped in butter. Bake at 400 degrees for 20 minutes, then reduce to 375 degrees. Bake until it is nicely browned, (about 10 minutes more). Turn onto a serving dish and serve with cream.

Trifle

Trifle, like Cornish pasties, can vary between the very nice and the very nasty. It is worth trying quite hard with it. I had two friends who made a habit of having trifle whenever they went out for a meal, and marking them from one to ten. They found as much variety as if they had had different desserts each time. They only awarded one trifle ten out of ten.

1 plain sponge round, make as recipe on p. 55
2 glasses Madeira
1 liqueur glass brandy
2 eggs
2 yolks
½ pt. milk
Vanilla essence
½ pt. lightly whipped cream
Raspberry jam (home-made, if possible)
¼ pt. double cream
4 oz. flaked almonds, toasted in the oven for 10 minutes
2 oz. castor sugar

Break up the sponge cake roughly into pieces about the size of a walnut. Soak in the madeira and brandy. If the liquids do not cover the cake, put in some more. Make a custard by blending the eggs, yolks and castor sugar in a blender. Tip into a double saucepan, and add the milk. Heat gently but do not boil. When it is thick, remove from the heat, add a couple of drops of vanilla essence, and allow to cool before folding in the whipped cream. Spread about 3 tablespoonsful of raspberry jam on the sponge cake, and top with custard. Allow to get cold and set, then lightly beat the ¼ pt. of double cream and spread on top. Decorate with toasted almonds.

Charlecote Mill, Hampton Lucy, Warwickshire.
This picturesque watermill on the River Avon dates from about 1740.

Rhubarb Crumble

1½ lb. rhubarb
6 oz. brown sugar
1 tsp. ground ginger
8 oz. wholewheat flour
2 oz. flaked almonds
4 oz. margarine
4 oz. brown sugar

Slice the rhubarb, and mix with the 6 oz. brown sugar, and ginger. Mix the crumble mixture in a bowl, combining the flour and almonds, and rubbing in the margarine and finally, the 4 oz. brown sugar. Tip the fruit into an oven proof dish. Top with the crumble. Bake at 350 degrees for 30 minutes.

Atholl Brose

This can be a drink for Hogmanay (Scottish New Year), or it can be a pudding. Here it is a pudding which you could, of course, have at a Hogmanay party.

3 oz. medium oatmeal
2 tblsps. thin honey
A glass of whisky
6 oz. whipped cream
1 tblsp. toasted oatmeal

Mix the oatmeal with water to a thick paste. Stand for half an hour. Press the meal over a seive with a silver spoon, and to the liquid which drains through, add the honey and the whisky. You should have half a pint of liquid approximately, fairly thick from the oatmeal paste. Fold half the cream into this mixture, and turn into glasses, adding a little of the oatmeal if it seems too thin. Top with the rest of the cream, and scatter toasted oatmeal on top.

Shrove Tuesday Pancakes

Shrove Tuesday is the last day before Lent, and is called that because it was the day when everyone was 'shriven', or had their sins forgiven ready for the forty days of fasting to follow. For the same reason, there was a tradition of party-giving on that day which we still keep up in the form of pancake races, and tossing pancakes for supper at home.

Make pancakes according to the recipe on p. 27. For quantities, 1 oz. wholewheat flour to a pancake, though for Pancake day, smaller pancakes are better, as you are only going to fill them with lemon juice and sugar. To toss them, make sure they are not stuck to the frying pan (and it is better to use a frying pan than a griddle for these as the edges may help you not to drop them). Shake the pancakes, and lower the pan to about knee level. Bring up to waist level, flicking as you do. Be sure the frying pan stays flat, ready to catch the turned pancake. Come to think of it, knowing how to play lacrosse or tennis may help. I don't think milling skills help here.

Bread Fritters

(Pain Perdu)

6 slices of stale white bread cut into patterns (circles, triangles and squares about 1/4 inch thick)
1 pt. custard, flavoured with 1/2 glass rum
1 tblsp. flour (white)
2 eggs

Soak the slices of bread in the rum-flavoured custard. Roll them one by one in the flour, then dip into the well beaten egg. Drop into deep frying oil and cook for 3 minutes. This is a delicious dessert, with a crisp crust of flour and egg, soft and aromatic in the centre.

Chocolate Gateau

8 oz. plain chocolate
6 eggs
8 oz. castor sugar
1 tblsp. brandy
1/2 pt. whipped cream
5 oz. sifted white unbleached flour
1 cup strong coffee
1 oz. butter
1 large egg
Pieces of chrystallized ginger

Cook 4 oz. chocolate with a dstsp. water to a thick cream. Cool down. Beat the eggs and sugar together. Stir in the flour and the chocolate mixture. Bake in a 8 inch cake tin at 375 degrees for 20-30 minutes. Make a chocolate butter icing with 4 oz. chocolate heated with coffee, gently, in a pan. When it is melted and creamy, beat the egg and softened butter together, and mix in. Add the brandy. Sandwich the cake with this. Top with whipped cream decorated with chrystallized ginger.

Crêpes à la Normande

Pancake batter, made as on *p. 27*
1 lb. cooking apples
1/2 tsp. cinnamon
3 oz. castor sugar
1 oz. blanched almonds
Calvados
Cream, whipped with a little sugar and vanilla essence

Stew the apples, sliced, peeled and cored, with cinnamon and castor sugar. Mix the nuts into the pancake batter, when it has stood for half an hour. Make the pancakes, and keep warm on a plate in a cool oven. Keep the apple purée warm on the side of the stove. When you want to serve them, put a filling of a little apple purée into each pancake, and fold over. Pour half a liqueur glass of calvados over each. Sprinkle with sugar and serve with whipped cream.

5. Tea Time Baking

Tea time recipes, not surprisingly, appeal to millers, who may be working long hours in a cold mill all day. Coming in to a slice of apple or walnut and raisin cake or a wholemeal scone can make a satisfying moment to look forward to, when the milling is finished, the sacks standing ready for delivery tomorrow, the mill turned off and peace and quiet restored. There is always something to be done while you are still at the mill, and that is what makes the life interesting. What the weather is doing, which can result in too much or too little water or wind, noises in one or other of the cog wheels, meaning you need to put in another wedge to make a better mesh in the old machinery, questions in your mind as to how the quality of this load of grain compares with the last, doubts as to the economics of taking on a big new order, involving delivery some distance away, little adjustments that need to be dealt with to make your sack hoist work more efficiently. All these are interesting problems which crop up all the time. Add to these the light in the morning on your mill stream or sails, and the many delights your eye is bound to rest on in a day at any time of the year, and it sounds idyllic. It isn't, of course. It can be cold, physically exhausting and financially very precarious. But one of the best things about it I know is coming home to something freshly baked for tea or supper, knowing that it is made from flour ground in the mill. The idea of this little book of recipes is to share some of these feelings with you.

Y Felin Mill Christmas Cake

Mike Hall grinds wholewheat and unbleached white flour and oatmeal at this delightful little mill at St. Dogmaels in Cardiganshire.

4 oz. dried apricots
4 oz. marzipan
3 eggs
4 oz. chopped walnuts
The rind and juice of
1 large orange
8 oz. wholewheat flour
6 oz. butter
6 oz. castor sugar
4 oz. glacé cherries (halved)
8 oz. sultanas
1 tsp. baking powder
2 tsps. ground cinnamon

Heat oven to 160 degrees C, (325 F), Gas 3.

Grease and line the cake tin. Snip apricots into quarters. Place in a basin and cover with boiling water. Roll the marzipan into marble-sized balls. Cream the butter and sugar. Beat eggs and add to butter and sugar a little at a time, beating after each addition. Drain the apricots and stir in with the cherries, walnuts, marzipan, orange juice (made up to ¼ pint with apricot liquor if necessary) and sultanas. Mix well. Sift the flour, baking powder and cinammon together and fold into the mixture. Place the mixture in the tin and smooth the top. Bake in centre of oven for 1 hour. Reduce heat to 150 degrees/300F/Gas 2 and cook for a further hour and 15 minutes to 1½ hours. Leave to cool, then turn out and store in a tin. Almond paste, ice and decorate as desired. This recipe is a firm family favourite, beautifully moist and crumbly. Will store up to 3 weeks in a tin or 6 weeks in the fridge in clingfilm.

Y Felin Mill, Cardiganshire, showing the overshot waterwheel, which turns 3 pairs of stones

Maud Foster Mill Fruit Cake

4 oz. margarine
6 oz. soft brown sugar
12 oz. mixed fruit
4 oz. glacé cherries
1 teacup of apple purée
2 beaten eggs
8 oz. wholemeal flour
2 tsps. baking powder

Boil in a pan margarine, sugar, fruit, cherries and apple purée. Remove from the heat and cool slightly, then add flour mixed with baking powder and beaten eggs, and mix well. Pour into a greased tin. Bang on the table to level. Bake about 50 to 60 minutes at 350 degrees.

Otterton Mill Walnut and Raisin Cake

8 oz. wholewheat flour
8 oz. margarine
1 small tsp. baking powder
6 oz. broken walnuts
10 oz. sultanas
8 oz. brown sugar
4 eggs

Melt the margarine and sugar together in a saucepan over a gentle heat. Mix together the dry ingredients and gradually add the melted margarine and sugar. Mix well. Put into a greased tin and cook at about 350 degrees for 1 hour.

Boardhouse Mill Birsay Biscuits

8 oz. Plain wholemeal flour
6 oz. sultanas
8 oz. butter/margarine
8 oz. sugar
3 oz. beremeal
1 egg
2 tsps. baking powder

Cream butter and sugar, add egg. Slowly add dry ingredients and sultanas. Roll out and cut out on floured board. Place on greased tray and bake in moderate oven for 15 minutes.

Felin Crewi Crunchy Bran Fingers

At this mill in Mid-Wales, Barry and Patti Partridge make 100% wholemeal and unbleached white flours, plain and self-raising, and their own bran and wheatgerm. This is one of the recipes they use in their cafe.

11 oz. wholemeal flour
1 oz. bran
8 oz. margarine or butter
4 oz. soft brown sugar
½ tsp. cinnamon

Cream margarine and sugar until very soft, then fold in bran, flour and spice. Mix well. Tip mixture into well-greased Swiss roll tin and level with palette knife. Press round edges with fingers. Mark into 18 fingers with knife and prick all over with a fork. Bake at about 350f. for 30 minutes. Leave to cool for 5 minutes, then carefully lift biscuits onto a cooling tray.

Little Salkeld Mill Apple Cake

For sponge base:
5 oz. wholewheat flour
4 oz. butter or vegetable margarine
1 dstsp. honey
2 eggs
A little water

For the top:
2 large apples (cooking or dessert)
1 tblsp. honey
1 tsp. cinnamon

Cream the fat with the honey and beat the eggs in gradually. Fold the flour into the creamed mixture, together with a little water to make a soft consistency. Pour into a greased and lined sandwich tin or swiss roll tin. Cut the apples into fine slices and arrange them in overlapping rows to cover the raw sponge mixture. Mix the cinnamon and honey together and sprinkle over the top of the apple. Bake at 375 degrees F (Gas Mark 5) for 45 minutes or until cooked.

Hoskens Mill Victoria Sponge Cake

6 oz. soft margarine
6 oz. sugar
6 oz. wholewheat flour
3½ tsps. baking powder
3 eggs
1 drop vanilla essence

Beat margarine and sugar together. Add the eggs and vanilla essence. Mix in flour and baking powder, add water if required. Cook at 325 degrees for 30 minutes in tins lined with greaseproof paper.

Little Salkeld Mill Malt Bread

1¼ lb. wholewheat flour
4 oz. rolled oats
2 oz. chopped walnuts
8 oz. sultanas or raisins
1 oz. fresh yeast or ½ oz. dried yeast
3 tblsps. malt extract
2 tsps. molasses
1 pt. warm water

Put all the dry ingredients and fruit into a large bowl. Dissolve the yeast in ¼ pt. of the warm water. To the remaining water add the molasses and malt extract. When the yeast is frothy add it to the dry ingredients together with the malty liquid. Mix it well and knead. Cover with a damp cloth and put it in a warm place to rise, then knead it again. Divide the dough into two and put into 1½ lb. loaf tins to prove. Bake at 450 degrees F (Gas Mark 8) for about 25 minutes, allowing the temperature to drop to about 400 degrees F (Gas Mark 6) during baking.

Otterton Mill Gingerbread

1 lb. flour
8 oz. syrup
8 oz. margarine vegetable
¼ pt. milk
A pinch of mixed spice
¼ tsp. bicarbonate of soda
8 oz. treacle
8 oz. brown sugar
3 eggs
A pinch of salt
½ tsp. ground ginger

Warm the milk and dissolve the margarine in it. Add treacle, syrup and the beaten eggs. Add to the dry ingredients which have been previously blended, and mix all well together. Put into a greased tin, and cook at 325 degrees for about an hour.

Little Salkeld Watermill Carob Cake

Carob is produced from the Locust bean. It is an excellent substitute for cocoa. Cocoa contains the stimulant caffeine and oxalic acid which prevents calcium being absorbed in the body. Carob is far richer in nutrients (iron, calcium and vitamins) and is highly digestible. St. John is said to have lived on it in the wilderness.

10 oz. wholewheat flour
2 tsps. baking powder
1 oz. carob powder
10 oz. vegetable margarine
2 tblsps. honey
2 eggs
3 oz. warm water

Cream the margarine and the honey. Add the eggs and beat to a light consistency. Add the flour and baking powder. Mix the carob with the warm water and add it to the mixture. Mix thoroughly. Put into two 8″ sponge tins and bake at 350 degrees (Gas Mark 4) for about half an hour. When cool cut each cake in half and sandwich with the icing. Cover the top and sides with the icing and sprinkle with flaked almonds.

Icing:
4 oz. butter
4 oz. honey
1 oz. soya flour
1 oz. carob powder
2 oz. water

Cream the butter and honey together and add the soya flour. Slowly add the carob powder and the water and mix well. The icing needs to be made in advance so that it can thicken.

Martha's Sugar-Free Prune and Banana Loaf

1 lb. prunes
2 oz. walnuts
1 lemon
½ tsp. ground cloves
3 eggs
A little water
½ tsp. ground nutmeg
2 oz. desiccated coconut
2 large bananas
6 oz. wholewheat flour
3 tsps. baking powder

(N.B. There is no fat in this, either).

Stew the prunes and walnuts with the spices, about ¼ pt. water and the juice of half the lemon. When the prunes are soft, stone them, and then liquidize the mixture, add the roughly chopped bananas, and the rest of the lemon juice. Stir in the coconut, and the flour and baking powder. Add the three egg yolks, beaten, and whisk the egg whites stiffly. Fold in with a metal spoon. Turn into a loaf tin, and bake at 375 degrees for 30 minutes.

Otterton Mill Chocolate Coconut Biscuits

8 oz. margarine
4 oz. sugar
¾ tsp. baking powder
6 oz. coconut
8 oz. wholewheat flour
2 oz. cocoa
For the icing:
8 tblsps. icing sugar
2 tblsps. cocoa
Boiling water

Cream the margarine and the sugar, and add the flour, coconut and cocoa. Mix to a firm dough and press into shallow, rectangular biscuit tins, well greased. Cook at 375 degrees for about 20 minutes. To make the icing, mix cocoa and icing sugar. Add boiling water gradually, about 2-3 tblsps., until a thick icing is made. Spread it on the hot chocolate biscuit when it comes out of the oven. Do not cut until it is cold, then cut into squares or rectangles.

Little Salkeld Wholewheat Crumpets

8 oz. wholewheat flour
1 tsp. salt
1 tsp. honey
½ oz. dried yeast
¼ pt. milk
8½ fl.oz. water

Heat the milk and water until just warm and add the yeast that has been creamed with the honey. Leave in a warm place until frothy. Sift the flour and salt into a bowl, add yeast liquid and mix well. Leave in a warm place for approx. 30 minutes until light and spongey. Oil metal biscuit cutters or crumpet rings and place on a greased griddle over a gentle heat. Spoon about ½″ of mixture into cutters and cook until bubbles rise to surface. Remove cutters and turn crumpets over to cook for approx. 2 minutes or until set.

Cann Mills Hot Cross Buns

1½ lb. 81% stoneground flour
½ oz. salt
3 oz. lard
2 oz. fresh yeast
3 oz. white sugar
1 egg
4 tsps. mixed spice
5 oz. currants
½ oz. mixed peel
¾ pt. approx. half water, half milk

Mix together flour, salt and mixed spice. Crumb in the fat, and add the egg. Add the yeast, sugar, water and milk having been well mixed beforehand. Leave to ferment, covered, in a warm place for 60 minutes. Knead lightly, mixing in the currants and peel in so doing. Divide the dough into 3 oz. pieces, mould into rolls and place onto a greased baking sheet. Leave covered in a warm place until well risen. Produce a mixture of 1½ oz. self-raising flour, ½ oz. fat, and then add milk until it is a piping consistency. Use a piping bag and using this mixture pipe crosses onto the buns. Bake at 425-450 degrees for 10-15 minutes. Make a strong sugar and water solution and brush this on the buns as soon as they come out of the oven.

Felin Crewi Bara Brith

1 lb. sultanas soaked in
12 oz. cold tea, orange or apple juice, overnight
12 oz. soft brown sugar
1 lb. 100% wholemeal self-raising flour
2 heaped tsps. mixed spice
2 eggs
Milk to mix.

Beat all the ingredients together to a sloppy consistency. Put into 2 large, or 3 small greased, lined loaf tins. Bake at 325 f. for 1–1½ hours. When cold, wrap in clingfilm and store for up to 3 weeks. Serve sliced and spread with butter.

Felin Crewi Welsh Cakes

6 oz. unbleached s.r. flour
4½ oz. lard
1 tblsp. sugar
4 oz. currants
1 egg
Water to mix

Rub fat into flour and add other ingredients to make a stiff dough. Roll out on a floured surface to a quarter of an inch. Cut into circles, using a tumbler. Welsh cakes should be cooked on a griddle. If you haven't one use a heavy non-stick frying pan. Pre-heat and cook about 2 minutes each side. Cool on a tea towel laid on a wire tray. Fold the tea towel over the cakes when finished to await buttering for tea time.

Downfield Windmill Chelsea Buns

Nigel Moon, at Downfield Windmill in Soham, Cambridgeshire, grinds English wheat, organically grown cereals in wheat, oats, rye and barley, and non-organic maize.

1 lb. wholemeal or brown flour
A pinch of salt
1 oz. yeast
1 tsp. ground cinnamon
½ oz. ground almonds
3 oz. brown sugar
3 oz. margarine
3 oz. currants
A little pineapple or lemon juice

Wash the currants and leave to soak in the fruit juice. Put flour, salt, ground cinnamon and ground almonds in a bowl. Get yeast going using a teaspooon of the sugar and when ready, add to the well-mixed dry ingredients in the bowl. Make dough in the usual way, and when proved roll out into two rectangles fairly thinly. Spread with small 'blobs' of margarine. Sprinkle with sugar, and lastly strain currants and spread on top. Now fold in three and seal ends. Give each of the folded rectangles a quarter turn, and roll out gently into two rectangles – not too thickly. This time roll up like a Swiss Roll. Cut off inch "wheels" and arrange on a greased baking tray. Cook about 15 minutes in a hot oven about 425 degrees or so. When cool decorate if you like with a little icing sugar and either poppy seeds or perhaps chopped nuts.

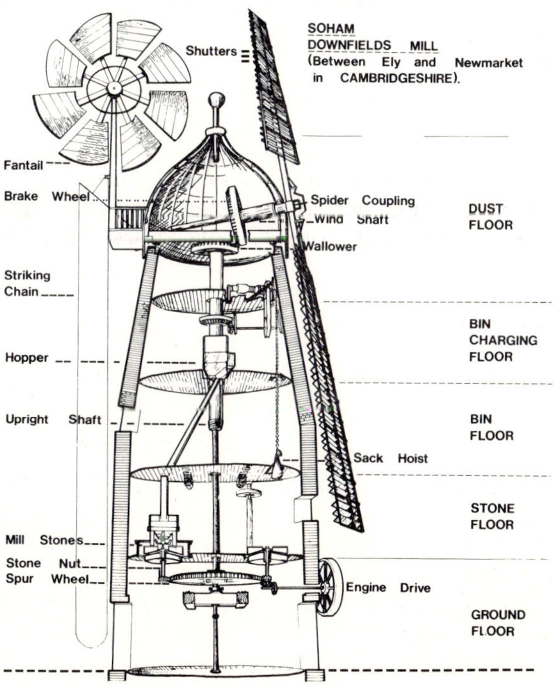

Mapledurham Mill Muesli Biscuits

4 oz. wholewheat flour
4 oz. muesli
2 tsps. baking powder
1 tsp. syrup
4 oz. margarine

Rub margarine into dry ingredients. Add syrup and mix well together. Roll into balls the size of walnuts. Place on a greased baking tray and flatten with a fork. Bake at 325 degrees or Gas Mark 3 for 10–15 minutes.

Maud Foster Mill Peanut Cookies

2 oz. washed salted peanuts
1 tblsp. golden syrup
1 oz. soft brown sugar
1½ oz. butter
3 oz. untreated white flour
Vanilla essence

Melt in a pan syrup, sugar and butter. Add vanilla essence to taste, add peanuts mixed with flour and mix all thoroughly. Put in small pieces on baking tray. Bake at 375 degrees for 12 minutes.

Tailpiece

Maxey Watermill's Pigmeal

Donald Stables grinds and processes corn at Maxey Mill, Peterborough for his herd of pigs. This is a satisfactory diet for the milking sow.

375 kgs. stoneground wheat
37 kgs. wheatfeed
25 kgs. white fishmeal
25 kgs. soya bean meal
6 kgs. soya oil
25 kgs. meat and bone meal

Plus vitamins and minerals as required.

The poet John Clare wrote about this mill, in his poem, 'The Fall of the Year'.

"The Summer's voice is still
Save the clacking of the mill
And the lowly-muttered thunder of the flood..."

List of Guild Members

Birsay, Orkney
Boardhouse Mill, Birsay, Orkney. Tel: 085672 363
Contact: Fergus Morrison (miller).
Open to the public: Yes, by appointment.
Power source: Overshot wheel from Boardhouse Burn.
Products: Beremeal (made from Hordeum Vulgare, an ancient form of barley grown in Orkney since 2000B.C., oatmeal, 100% wholemeal biscuit flour.
Grist: Beremeal organically grown by miller. Oats and wheat from cornmerchants.
History: Built in 1873, the last working watermill in Orkney. The mill is the only producer of beremeal.

Blackland, near Calne, Wilts.
Mill Farm, Blackland, near Calne, Wilts. Tel: Calne 814507.
Contact: Mr and Mrs H. D. Hosken.
Power source: breast-shot water wheel, 18 ft. diameter.
Products: strong Baker's grade 100% stoneground flour, malted wheat flakes.
History: On the site of a monastic mill dating from 1215, the present buildings, about 1800.
Other details: 3 pairs French burr stones.

Bordon, Hants.
Headley Mill, Bordon, Hants. Tel: (04203) 2031.
Contact: John Ellis.
Open to the public: By appointment. (Specially educational groups).
Products: 100% wholewheat flour, maize, barley, crushed and rolled oats for animal feed.
History: A Saxon mill. The mill pond was enlarged in 1272. The manor mill of Bishops Sutton. Some of the building is pre-16th century, with the external parts being Tudor and late eighteenth century. It has been in the same family since 1914.
Other details: 3 pairs of French burr stones, and 1 of Derby peaks. The head of water is 7½ ft. from a 4 acre pond.

Boston, Lincs.
The Maud Foster Mill, Boston, Lincs. Tel: 0205 52188.
Contact: James Waterfield (miller).
Open to the public: all the year round, Sundays 2-5.
Power source: 5 patent sails regulated from the balcony encircling the 3rd floor.
Products: 100% wholemeal, 85% brown, untreated white, self raising 100% and white, pancake flour, rye flour, buckwheat flour, wheat flakes, oat flakes, semolina and bran; mostly organic.
History: Built in 1819 for Isaac & Thomas Reckitt for £1,826. Ceased working in 1947. Restored in 1987.
Other details: The tallest working windmill in Britain. 3 pairs stones, a corn cleaner, flour dresser, oat roller and mixer, and a pair of electrically driven stones for when there is no wind.

Budleigh Salterton, Devon.
Otterton Mill, near Budleigh Salterton, EX9 7HG. Tel: Colaton Raleigh (0395) 68521/68031.
Contact: Desna Greenhow (miller).
Open to the public: daily, 1030-1730 (1400-1700 winter weekends), all the year round.
Power source: breast-shot water wheel.
Products: wholemeal wheat flour, own label baked goods using own flour.
Grist: grain is bought from farmers or co-operatives and only English wheat is used, aiming for a protein of 12%.
History: A pre-Conquest mill, then the manor mill for Otterton Priory. Partly re-built in 1850, the core and some of the machinery is older. Restored in 1977.
Other details: 2 pairs French burr stones, with rhymed dedications on them. 1 pair composition stones.

Clapton, Crewkerne, Somerset.
Clapton Mill, Clapton, Crewkerne, Somerset. Tel: 0460 73124.
Contact: John Lockyer (miller).
Power source: 21 ft. diameter water wheel.
History: Built in 1864, on a site possibly dating back to 1200. 5 generations of owner millers.

Hampton Lucy, Warwicks.
Charlecote Mill, Hampton Lucy, Warwick CV35 8BB. Tel: Stratford upon Avon (0789) 842072.
Contact: John Bedington (miller).
Open to the public: by appointment, to purchasers of flour, normal office hours, telephone first.
Power source: undershot waterwheel.
Products: wholemeal wheat flours – *All English for Bread* (AEB); *All English for Chapattis* (AEC); *Bakers' Blend* (BB);· *Organic* (O). Some oats and barley for domestic animal feed.
Grist: the Chapatti blend is best with a vitreous Avalon; the other blends are often Avalon (the most common Midland variety) but are bought according to performance, not variety. Protein and Hagberg tests are done as a matter of course, but a test bake is also the norm. The Baker's Blend is produced at 12.5% protein; if the English wheats cannot supply this, Canadian is added to the grist. The AEC is at least 9% protein and the AEB (in reality a household general purpose flour) at least 11%, as is the Organic. 8% of output is organic. Grain is purchased from dealers (25%) and direct from farmers.
History: A pre-Conquest mill, valued in Domesday at 6s. 8d. The present building is about 1740, with a later section behind.
Other details: The studded doors are a feature of Warwickshire watermills.

Harbertonford, Devon.
Crowdy Mill, Harbertonford, Totnes. TQ9 7HU. Tel: Harbertonford (080 423) 340.
Contacts: Martin Watts (miller) & Don Barnes (owner).
Open to the public: to flour purchasers, working weekdays, 08.30–16.30; other times by appointment only.
Power source: two overshot waterwheels.
Products: wholemeal wheat, Standard English/Organic/Strong; 85% wheat, Standard English/Organic; unbleached white wheat, Standard English; rye wholemeal.
Grist: usually grinding Avalon, Moulin or similar, Timmo and Springs if available. 12% protein for the strong blend (mainly for bakers), achieved by up to 35% Canadian admixture if English wheat not up to scratch. Most grain bought from merchants, about 5% direct from farmers.
History: A mill on the site for 700 years, the present mill was restored in 1984.
Other details: three sets of stones.

Little Salkeld, Cumbria.
The Watermill, Little Salkeld, Penrith, CA10 1NN. Tel: Langwathby (076 881) 523.
Contact: Nicolas Jones (miller).
Open to the public: shop open Mon-Fri 0930-1230, 1430-1730; the mill open by appointment only.
Power source: overshot waterwheels.
Products: full range of flours and meals from organically grown crops: 100% and 85% plain and self-raising wheat flours, 100% rye flour, 85% barley flour, a special blend (Water mill) including soya, sunflower and sesame, and Granarius, a granary type. In addition, there are lines in bran, goat-food, dog meal and other by-products. Oatmeals are milled for them, from organic crops. English grans are used.
Grist: Organic crops are bought from farmers, and Soil Association Symbol wheats are used. Maris Widgeon, Maris Dove, Timmo, Sicco and Bouquet are the varieties preferred. Purchases are not by test results as much as by the test baking of a loaf. A variety of grinds – extra fine, medium fine (their standard) or coarse. Bread makers who know the value (for lightness) of a fine grind will like to know this may be requested.
History: The third mill at Little Salkeld, the present one built 200 years ago by the Atkinson family, who milled here for four centuries.
Other details: French burr stones. The wider water wheel (4ft. 9in. across) develops up to 15 h.p.

Mapledurham, near Reading, Oxon.
Mapledurham Mill, Mapledurham Estate, near Reading.
Contact: Mildred Cookson (miller).
Open to the public: Easter-end September, Sats and Suns, 12.30-5.30. Rest of year Suns 2-4.
Power source: undershot water wheel, 12 ft. in diameter, driven by the River Thames.
Products: 100% wholemeal, 81% brown, semolina and bran.
History: A Domesday mill. The fifteenth century building can still be identified, as can additions in 1670 and 1700, forming the mill as it is today. The last working water mill on the River Thames.
Other details: 2 pairs French burr stones in use, 2 more used for demonstrations.

Maxey, Peterborough, Cambs.
Maxey Mill, Mill House, Maxey, Peterborough, Cambs. PE6 9EZ.
Contact: Donald Stables.
Open to the public: no.
Power source: wooden clasp arm breast shot water wheel.
Product: pig food.
History: Built in 1779 on a site dating back to the 12th century.
Other details: 2 pairs stones, one Garner carborundums, the other Derby peaks.

Penegoes, Mid-Wales
Felin Crewi Mill, Penegoes, Machynlleth, Powys SY20 8NH. Tel: 0654 3113
Contacts: Barry and Patti Partridge (owners)
Open to the public: Throughout the year, Easter-end September. every day, October-Easter, Monday-Friday.
Power source: Breast shot wheel.
Products: 100% wholemeal and unbleached white flour, plain and self-raising. Wheat germ, bran, and own muesli.
Grist: English wheat from grain merchants.
History: Built in 1650 as a fulling mill, it was converted to a corn mill in the eighteenth century, and an oat kiln built.
Other details: 2 sets of French burr stones, 1 in use. Disabled access to ground and first floor.

Rea Valley Mills.
Claybury Mill, Claybury Mortimer, Salop DY14 8QG. Tel: 0299 270034.
Newnham Mill, Newnham Bridge, Tenbury Wells, Hereford & Worcester.
Tel: 058479 494.
Contact: Jim Bartlett.
Open to the public: By appointment.
Power source: undershot water wheels.
Products: 100% wholewheat, chappati flour. Claybury: brown flour, unbleached white flour.
Grist: Bought from corn merchants, by protein and Hagbert results, aiming for 11% protein. Often Avalon. Foreign wheats added to bring up protein level if necessary.
History: Newnham Mill is a brick, eighteenth century building. Renovated in 1928, it fell into disuse after the Second World War. Restored in the seventies.

Ravenglass, Cumbria.
Muncaster Mill, Ravenglass, Cumbria. CA18 1ST. Tel: Ravenglass (06577) 232.
Contact: Peter Ellis (miller); The Eskdale (Cumbria) Trust (owners).
Open to the public: daily, except Sats, April, May and Sept. 1100-1700; June, July, Aug. 1000 1800; at other times by appointment.
Power source: overshot waterwheel.
Products: wholemeal wheatflour (coarse and fine grinds), 85% wheat flour, unbleached white wheat flour; wholewheat semolina, bran and cracked wheat. Both organic and inorganic flours are produced, though the majority have bought the former.
Grist: the bulk comes from corn merchants, with some from a milling colleague, Maris Widgeon and Avalon being the preferred varieties. 10%-11% protein is aimed for but this is not buttressed by use of foreign grain.
History: Probably on or close to the site of the manor mill of Muncaster. In 1470 the rent was £3 pa. The present building is eighteenth century. Restored in 1977.
*Other details:*French burr stones, Peak and shelling stones. A two-storey oatmeal mill.

St Dogmael's, Dyfed.
Y Felin, Mill Street, St Dogmael's, Cardigan SA43 3DY. Tel: Cardigan (0239) 613999.
Contact: Michael and Jane Hall.
Open to the public: through the summer, daily 1030-1730, through the winter, on weekdays only.
Power source and technical details: overshot water wheel.
Products: 100% and 85% and unbleached white wheat flours; rye flour and barley meal; a granary type malted flour; seed and herb wholemeal wheat flour; bran and semolina.
Grist: mostly bought through merchants, aiming at 11% minimum protein but not using foreign grain.
History: A mediaeval abbey mill.

Shaftesbury, Dorset.
N. R. Stoate & Sons, Cann Mill, Shaftesbury, Dorset. SP7 0BL. Tel: Shaftesbury (0747) 52475.
Contacts: Norman and Michael Stoate.
Products: A full range of plain, organic, self-raising and extra-strong flours available in 100% and 81% extraction, also 'Maltstar', (a granary type flour) and rye flour.
Grist: using largely Wessex crops for their grist, a high protein level is aimed for and achieved.
Other details: 5 pairs French burr stones.

Skenfrith, Gwent.
Skenfrith Mills, near Abergavenny, Gwent. Tel: (060084) 651.
Contact: Malcolm Edwards (miller).
Open to the public: no.
Power source: Undershot wheel off the River Monnow.
Products: 100% whole wheat, 85% brown flour, barley and oatmeal for animal feed.
Grist: Local English wheat, with a small proportion of Canadian wheat. Some organic wheat.
History: Recorded in 1300, when it served a fortified castle. The core of the mill dates from 1500, with additions in 1650 and 1867.
Other details: 2 pairs French quartz composition stones.

Soham, Cambridgeshire.
Downfield Windmill, Fordham Road, Soham, Cambridgeshire. Tel: Ely (0353) 720333.
Contact: Nigel Moon (miller), home number, Leicester (0533) 707625.
Open to the public: every Sunday and bank holiday Monday, 1100-1700.
Power source and technical details: windmill.
Products: wholemeal and brown wheat flours, organic and standard: organic rye, barley and oat meals; maize meal for feed; wheat bran.
Grist: though mostly supplied by merchants, it is bought from farmers where possible, normally Avalon or Brimstone, at a protein level of 11-12%. Gluten is sold at the mill to home bakers who wish to aim for a lighter loaf.
History: Started as a smock mill in 1726, and was gradually altered to its present form.
Other details: This is a four-storied brick tower mill. 3 pairs of stones.